The

BELIEVER'S IDENTITY

DEVOTIONAL HANDBOOK

120 "I AM" STATEMENTS OF A CHRISTIAN

The

BELIEVER'S IDENTITY
DEVOTIONAL HANDBOOK

120 "I AM" STATEMENTS OF A CHRISTIAN

J. Nicole Williamson

KING'S LANTERN
PUBLISHING

The Believer's Identity Devotional Handbook
Copyright © 2016 J. Nicole Williamson

King's Lantern Publishing

Allen, TX

www.kingslantern.com

Printed in the United States of America.

ISBN-10 098513965X

ISBN-13 978-0-9851396-5-0

Scripture quotations referenced are individually noted and used by permission.

Cover design by J. Nicole Williamson

Senior Editor: Ken Williamson

DEDICATION

To the sons and daughters of God everywhere. May you know and experience the joy and truth of who you are in Christ. May you declare it with confidence for there is power in your words of agreement with God.

You are an eternal being in a mortal body with a divine purpose on earth for such a time as this. You are here by divine intention! May you live fully for Him who has loved you and gave Himself for you. May you step confidently into the vast and radiant qualities of the identity you carry as the Body of the Lord Jesus Christ. May you shine with Heaven's glory in your soul.

CONTENTS

INTRODUCTION

It is time for the Body of Christ to rise and shine with divine presence and power for healing nations. We are here for a purpose and for such a time as this. For this we must know our God and who we are in Him. We must change how we think about who we are, for how we think determines how we show up in life, relationships, and calling. We must think as He thinks about our identity and who He is in us.

Since the Garden of Eden, Satan has tried to twist, demean, and distort how we view God and ourselves as His children. He wants to cloak our radiant identity in Him. Satan fears our awakening to the glory we carry; he fears the transforming light that shines through us to dispel darkness. He works craftily so that we live far below what God intends. He works to steal our power and authority, to cripple our movement, and cloud our minds. He uses messages scripted in hell to accuse and assault us on a daily basis through broken relationships, worldly philosophy, personal failures, and even false religious structures.

Nevertheless, we are not captive to such schemes! We have the truth and the truth has set us free. It is time to replace Satan's lies with the truth about God and who Christ is in us!

New birth in the Messiah brings us out of old paradigms of death and into a glorious new and living way of being. This includes new perspectives and new actions! As believers in Jesus (Yeshua), we must see ourselves wholly in Him, of Him, and as a part of Him. He is our identity. He is the Second Adam who restores us fully to being the image of God on Earth. Only as we fully immerse our life and understanding of being conformed to His likeness can we fulfill our Kingdom purpose on Earth.

I John 4:17 says, "As He is, so also are we in this world." This statement is an important truth regarding our identity as believers in the Messiah. The term "identity" refers to the set of qualities that *define* a thing or person and the characteristics by which they are known.

God Declares His Identity

God declares His own identity over and over throughout Scripture through many descriptive names. Each name bears a special quality or characteristic that expresses who God is and how He manifests Himself to this world, towards His people, and against His enemies. They express how He shows up! There are well over 700 scriptural names and descriptions of how God reveals Himself, some say there are thousands.

Here are just a few of those names and descriptions:

I Am that I Am

El Shaddai (Many Breasted One)

Elohim (God, Triune One)

Yahweh (Jehovah, Lord)

Adonai (Lord)

Creator

God of Israel

Jehovah-Shalom (God of Peace)

Jehovah-Rapha (God who Heals me)

Jehovah-Shamma (the Lord is there)

Jehovah-Tsidkenu (the Lord our righteousness)

Jehovah-Makeddish (the Lord who sanctifies)

Jehovah-Father of Lights

God of Hope

Abba Father

Judge of All

Living Elohim (God)

God of Comfort

Lifter of my head

Lord of Sabaoth (Hosts)

Mighty Warrior

Beginning and End

Alpha and Omega

Messiah (Savior)

Rock

Redeemer

The Lord is my Light

The Lord is my Salvation

Hashem is Gracious

The Lord who sanctifies me

The Lord is my Shepherd

Yahweh is Holy

Yahweh is Righteous

The Lord is my Banner

God of Truth

Yeshua is The Way

Yeshua is The Truth

Yeshua is The Life

The Light

Bread of Heaven

Only Wise God

Immutable God

Faithful and True

King of Glory

Son of Man

Son of God

Anointed One

Holy Child	Spirit of Holiness
Ruler of the Nations	Consuming Fire
Desire of the Nations	Spirit of Truth
Comforter	Spirit of Grace
Teacher	Spirit of Burning
Helper	Spirit of Wisdom

Declaring Our Identity in Christ

Only as we begin to know our God and Creator can we truly begin to know our own identity in Him. To make an "I am" declaration from Scripture about ourselves is not arrogance or self-focus. Rather, it is about affirming who Christ is in us and who we are as God's children who bear His image. It is about declaring truth against the voices that seek to cloud the brilliant identity we carry with Kingdom authority over the enemy.

Declarations of truth are powerful for bringing down strongholds and breaking the wrong mental images we may still carry as Christians. Words carry the power of life and death. It is time to dispel darkness and empower life through agreement with God in what we think and say…and thus do.

As the Body of Christ, it is time to stop apologizing for who we are, stop cowering to darkness, stop allowing unbelieving mindsets to rule us. It is time to stop allowing chaos to wreak havoc in our lives, families, communities, and nation. It is time to walk in truth and break out of the tiny boxes of understanding we may have put ourselves in — boxes that hinder our full development as sons of glory and the glorious Bride of Christ.

What we believe, consciously or unconsciously, becomes our "default" mindset — our "go to" mode of thinking in how we live, respond, and show up in our day. It is time to upgrade our default mode from fear and limitations to victory and divine possibilities!

The following pages of declarations are a way to reinforce truth about who we are in the Messiah and the purposeful life we are called to live in Him. I have also chosen to use a few of the Hebrew terms and names for God in this book as a way to reinforce our identity of being children of the *God of Israel*. Many in Western Christianity have not fully understood that we are grafted into a covenant that God gave to *Israel* through Yeshua who then extended it to the whole world…to us. Sometimes just saying something in a different way can jar us out of an old way of seeing

13

something and awaken us to a new perspective. And, too, using terms that refer to God in more personal terms trains our thoughts of Him in meaningful ways.

Some of the terms you will see scattered throughout the book include:

- *Abba* (Dad, Papa)

- *Adonai* (Lord)

- *Elohim* (God, Triune One)

- *Yeshua* (Jesus' Hebrew name, Yahushua: "salvation is from Yahweh")

- *Hashem* ("The Name." Hashem is another Jewish way of saying "Dad" and is a term used for God's name as both intimate and yet respectful and is what Jewish culture uses in place of the Holy Name, Yahweh.)

Using this Devotional

As you read through these affirmations of "being" do so prayerfully, letting each one sink deep into your heart, thoughts, and spirit. These life transforming statements are best when not only read, but declared OUT LOUD. This is who you are! Believe it! Say it! Declare it with confidence because of the blood of Jesus. Let them energize your spirit and thoughts throughout the day; let them connect you to Christ in a new way.

Ask Holy Spirit to expose any negative or limiting mindset in you; then command it to be broken, uprooted, and to leave you in Jesus' name. Ask Holy Spirit to reveal these truths to you personally and how He wants you to walk in them through your life and calling in divine purpose. You can also use this daily devotional as a springboard for personal study as you dig deeper into God's Word regarding each day's statement.

Another great way to use this book is at family mealtimes. It is a great way to engage meaningful conversations about God, and about who you and your family are in Christ. Use it to train the next generation! Or you can use it for a group study with friends, taking different declarations each week for studying and exploring their rich truths together.

It is time to fully know who we are as believers in Yeshua the Messiah, and as the children of Adonai who show up in this world as His glorious lights. People are waiting for the light that dispels darkness. They are waiting for freedom.

They are waiting for Christ in you and me.

DAY 1

I AM ACCEPTED OF GOD

To the praise of the glory of His grace by which He has made us accepted in the Beloved. (Eph. 1:6 NKJV)

Acceptance is a desire of every human heart. Acceptance is the acknowledgement and approval of someone who is received with recognized value. God receives me with great value to Himself. Sin brought the devastating experience of rejection and condemnation to the human heart, but divine love and grace through the cross returns me to complete acceptance in Christ.

Being accepted of God means that He does not reject me or shun me. Rather, He lovingly invites me to come to Him always, no matter what my past has been…no matter the current mistakes I make. In Christ I am fully accepted and received with love. I am desired by God. I am not rejected. His arms are open and His shining face is turned towards me.

Abba, help me to experience fully the unerring truth that I am accepted by You, and that I am acceptable in Your sight. Teach me to draw the affirmation of who I am from Your perspective and thoughts towards me, and not from any other's broken filters or dark opinions. Show me any place today where I do not accept myself and exchange it for the truth that I am accepted — a truth that sets me free. Father, show me who else needs to hear those words of acceptance today.

DAY 2

I AM ACCOMPANIED BY ANGELS

For He shall give His angels charge over you, to keep you in all your ways. (Ps. 91:11 KJV)

This world is more than what the natural eyes see. Dark forces are all around but so are the hosts of God's angels. They are sent to help me do Father's will. Angels are assigned to minister salvation, healing, comfort, help, and deliverance to me. They minister revelation and strength to me from God. Angels are assigned to my life by God from the moment I am conceived and brought into this world. They are with me always, even though I may not see them. They are given charge to keep me.

As a believer, I am accompanied by Heaven's messengers of fire. Scriptures show how angels advance the way of God's people for fulfilling divine purpose: they bring breakthrough, they war in the heavenlies on behalf of the prayers of God's people, and they speak to people in dreams. So, too, God sends His angels to advance my way in divine purpose, to bring me breakthrough, and heavenly insights into the will of God for me.

Abba Father, thank You for the ministry of angels to my life!

DAY 3
I AM AN ARROW IN MY FATHER'S HANDS

Children are a gift from the Lord; they are a reward from Him.
Children born to a young man are like arrows in a warrior's hands.
How joyful is the man whose quiver is full of them! He will not be
put to shame when he confronts his accusers at the city gates.
(Ps. 127:3-4 NLT)

As Hashem's child, my life is a reward to Him. My Heavenly Father is a Warrior and I am an arrow in His hand for accomplishing His will on Earth. He has a specific target of divine purpose He wants to use my life for in destroying works of darkness and bringing people to His love and liberty. My gift to Him as His child is a willing heart that surrenders to His refining work, intimate training, and loving guidance. These polish me to fly far and straight on the wings of His Holy Spirit to hit the target of His purpose for me, and to display His goodness in the Earth. He keeps me close to Him in His quiver and then sends me on assignment.

Abba, what a glory it is to be an arrow in Your hand, to be released with purpose into destiny. Help me to not resist Your training and not hold back in doing what You desire of me. You have fashioned me in a specific way to accomplish a specific task. What is the target You want to hit through my life today? Where do You want to send me today?

DAY 4
I AM ANOINTED BY GOD

But You have made me as strong as a wild ox. You have anointed me
with the finest [fresh] oil. (Ps. 92:10 NLT)

To anoint means to smear with oil; oil makes things work smoothly and optimally with full power. Here, the ox is a symbol of strength. I need inner strength for both the divine work I am given and the warfare I experience in life. And so He gives me fresh oil of His Spirit — the energizing power of His presence that renews my spirit and soul for movement with strength when I feel I have none. His anointing empowers me to forge through adversity and persevere through difficulties to obtain victory when all seems impossible.

In the Old Testament, David was a shepherd and well understood the importance of oil on a sheep's head to heal infections and protect it from harassing flies. Jesus knows I need oil on my head to heal my mind and empower my perspectives, and to protect me from the harassing thoughts sent from the enemy. David also understood the need for divine strength with strategy against enemies who were bigger and stronger than himself. He knew that true power for victory in war came from God, and for that he needed fresh oil from Heaven.

Abba, thank You for Your fresh empowerment that makes me strong when I am weary. Yesterday's strength is gone; I need fresh oil today that heals my mind, defeats the enemy, and empowers me to advance triumphantly. Anoint my head and fill me with fresh oil today.

DAY 5
I AM ANOINTED TO BRING GOOD NEWS

The Spirit of the Lord God is upon me, because the Lord has anointed
me to bring good news to the afflicted. (Isa. 61:1a HCSB)

God anoints me with divine power to be His messenger. I may be timid by nature, or not, but Yeshua certainly is not! He is bold and has a message from the Father that He wants to minister to others. And so He anoints me with a supernatural ability to minister God's message of hope to others, including words of wisdom and knowledge. The work of the cross has given me resurrection life and power to declare the good news of Christ. God wants people to know that He desires to restore them, heal them, deliver them, sustain them, and give them new life. And He wants me to deliver that message. His message is not in mere words, but it comes with demonstration of power to heal, encourage, and set free.

Father, who do You want me to speak to today and bring the demonstration of Your love, goodness, and power?

DAY 6
I AM ARMED FOR WAR

For the weapons of our warfare are not carnal but mighty in God for
pulling down strongholds, casting down arguments and every high thing
that exalts itself against the knowledge of God, bringing every thought

into captivity to the obedience of Christ. (2 Cor. 10:4-5 NKJV)

War is conflict. We live in a world at war — a spiritual conflict between darkness and light. This warfare is not with flesh and blood but with spiritual forces that work to kill, steal and destroy life. It is a war played out in the hearts and minds of mankind. It is a war we win through the power of the cross and resurrection of Jesus. It is a war that requires spiritual armor and weapons with divine counsel and strategy.

For this war I am given spiritual weapons that are effective for victory. These weapons are not manmade but are weapons of the Spirit — the Name of Jesus, the Word of God, which is truth and light, and the anointing of the Spirit. I have the weapons of prayer and praise. With these I also bring every thought captive to the obedience of Christ. Jesus also gives me armor to protect my heart, mind, and emotions with love, righteousness, truth, salvation, and peace. He gives me what I need to win; He also teaches my hands to war. As I seek His counsel for each battle and persevere with courage, I win with Him.

Jesus, thank You that You empower me by the Holy Spirit to be victorious in the battles I face on Earth. What thoughts do I need to bring to You now? What armor do I need to put on that I haven't yet? What weapon do I need to pick up today?

DAY 7

I AM AS HE IS

Herein is our love made perfect, that we may have boldness in the
day of judgment: because as He is, so are we in this world.
(1 John 4:17 KJV)

Yeshua perfects me in His love. Being perfect is not about performance and personal perfectionism, but about the completeness (nothing lacking, nothing missing) that Yeshua brings to my life. He is the Complete One, and in Him I live and move and have my being, and so I am whole — complete, nothing lacking, nothing missing. I am not substandard, deficient, or inferior. I am loved and am being conformed to the pattern of His love in all my ways by His presence with me.

His love shapes my thoughts with peace and courage, my attitude with patience, and my vision with hope. His love drives away fear and makes me bold. He works in my life through the power of His blood, death, and resurrection. He makes me stand confident before the throne of grace now, as well as before the throne of God in the day of judgment when all things are brought before Him who is the Judge of All. There I will stand complete in Christ's love.

Yeshua, make me as You are. Perfect me in Your love. Where does love need to be refined in my life today?

DAY 8

I AM A BEARER OF DIVINE IMAGE

So God created man in His own image; in the image of God He created him; male and female He created them. (Gen. 1:27 NKJV)

At creation, Elohim laced beautiful qualities of His own likeness into mankind. Humanity was unique from all the rest of creation. As a human being made in His image, I have attributes of intellect, spiritual capacity, creativity, vision and judgment laced within me. They have a purpose in my development as His child. And like all capacities, I learn to grow in them through intentional engagement with my spiritual senses and personal abilities. Even my gender is part of His likeness that He gave me. Though God is neither male nor female, in Him are both maternal and paternal attributes.

I was created intentionally and intricately by God to bear His likeness and represent Him on Earth, to labor with Him and advance His Kingdom of Light in a world of darkness. It is the cross that restores full capacity in me. Jesus teaches me to steward Elohim's image in me with purpose.

Abba Father, I desire to bring You glory, and to fulfill the very purpose for which I am called. Thank You for life and giving me Your likeness. What spiritual capacities or attributes do You want me to develop today?

DAY 9

I AM A BELIEVER IN JESUS

Jesus answered, "The work of God is this: to believe in the one He has sent." (John 6:29 NIV)

To believe something is to be persuaded and confident that it is true. It is to put one's trust in it as being so. Jesus' work from Father was on the cross to take my curse and give me new life. My work is to believe in Him, being confident that He is who He says He is and so live my life accordingly in intimacy with Him.

"Work" refers to the intentional actions I engage for prospering something as a matter of business, namely, the Father's business. The Father's business is to have a family of heirs who are in intimate relationship with Himself; this was the reason for the cross and resurrection of His Son, Jesus. My work in this matter is to take intentional actions to prosper my faith in God and in Jesus. Believing in Jesus is the work Father has given me on Earth — a faith that advances His Kingdom, governs in life, unites Heaven and Earth, and spreads the good news of His love and power to those I encounter on my journey.

Satan's self-appointed work is to cause me to doubt, to not believe, to mistrust, and to not take purposeful action. He tries with craftiness to inspire an unbelieving heart in me, which God says is an evil heart.

Abba, thank You for Jesus. I am a believer in Your Son! Grant me unwavering faith! What purposeful action of faith do You want me to take today?

DAY 10

I AM BEAUTIFUL

You are as beautiful as Tirzah, my darling, you are as… lovely as Jerusalem. (Song of Songs 6:4 NASB)

Some people would not call themselves beautiful, but beautiful is how Jesus sees us. In ancient Israel, Tirzah and Jerusalem were both royal cities held in high esteem. Tirzah means "She is my delight," while Jerusalem was the "apple of God's eye" and was called the city of the Great King. In this verse, this was how the king saw his bride — beautiful, royal, and the delight of his heart. And she was his.

This is how the King of Kings sees me; I am His delight and the apple of His eye. I am highly esteemed by Him; I am His. I am the glorious darling of His affections who carries His authority. Satan accuses and slanders me; he tries to demean my identity and trash how I see myself. But Jesus sees me as stunning, and He alone is truth and speaks truth. It is important that I see myself in His truth for truth sets me free. Seeing myself as beautiful in Him empowers me to step up and stand tall with courage that "I can do all things through Him." Thinking I am "lesser than," not good enough, or ugly causes me to step down and shrink back with an already defeated mindset. Such thinking has no place in the mind of royalty.

Jesus, thank You for making me beautiful and royal in Your love. Show me any place today where my thinking is not like Yours, where

I'm slumping and shrinking where I need to be standing regally at Your side, carrying Your authority as being Yours.

DAY 11
I AM BLESSED OF GOD

Blessed be the God and Father of our Lord Jesus Christ, who has blessed us with every spiritual blessing in the heavenly places in Christ.
(Eph. 1:3 NKJV)

The blessing of God is His tangible favor released to make His children prosper in every possible way. God wants me as His child to advance and succeed in the purposes He has for me. In ancient Israel, kings and priests were commanded to declare blessings on His people so they would prosper. Fathers would bless their wives and children so they would prosper. There is power in the spoken blessing! The cross and resurrection of Christ releases to me Abba's full blessings on my life for prospering in every way. "Blessed" is His decree over me.

I am no longer cursed under sin; I am blessed in Yeshua. Glory, grace, deliverance, wisdom, and healthy relationships, are just a few of those blessings. There are countless more. I don't have to beg for blessings; they are freely given me in Christ. Wisdom is mine. The counsel of God is mine. Healing is mine. And the presence of God is promised to be with me. Along with receiving blessings there also comes responsibility to be a blessing to others through what I am given in Christ. I am not to be a waster nor a hoarder of the blessings He has given me; I am blessed to be a blessing.

Father, thank You for Your blessings. What blessing have You given me that I am not fully walking in? How do You want me to bless another today with what You have given me?

DAY 12
I AM BUILT AS A SPIRITUAL HOUSE

You also, like living stones, are being built into a spiritual house to be a holy priesthood, offering spiritual sacrifices acceptable to God through Jesus Christ. (1 Pet. 2:5 NIV)

A spiritual house speaks of a spiritual family. In Christ, I am part of a spiritual family that He is building in the Earth to bring many sons and daughters to glory. It is a family of worshipers who worship Father in spirit and truth; they are connected together with a kindred heart. I am part of a family that stands daily in His presence ministering to Him with sacrifices of joy, praise, prayer, and worship. It is a family who loves and honors the Father because these are due Him.

Each one in this family is like a fiery gemstone; each carrying a spirit that burns with holy passion and each one holding a valuable and supportive place together for creating a welcoming place for God's presence in the Earth. It is a family filled with God's glory.

Father, thank You for making me a part of this flaming family of worshipers! Teach me to connect with my brothers and sisters to make a living dwelling place for You in the Earth. How do You want me to be a part of welcoming Your presence into my sphere of influence today?

DAY 13
I AM A CARRIER OF DIVINE PURPOSE

But He said to them, "I must preach the kingdom of God to the other cities, for I was sent for this purpose." (Luke 4:43 NASB)

As Hashem's child, I carry within my spiritual DNA the Divine Presence and thus His purposes on Earth. The Father sent Yeshua to destroy the works of the devil and bring us to Himself. As Yeshua's body, I, too, am sent to do the will of the Father in my generation. It is a purpose given with divine presence and power to preach His name, heal the sick, deliver from demonic oppression, and restore hearts.

Father wants His Kingdom and glory to cover the Earth that He created for His pleasure, a world that Satan wants to destroy. I am here to the effect my Father's good desires for my home and nation through the power of Yeshua's blood and presence of the Holy Spirit.

Scripture says that David served the purpose of God in his generation, that John the Baptist "completed his course," and that Paul had a race to run and he ran it with all his heart. Everything else to Paul was like dung compared to a life lived with Christ and for the cause of Christ. Each of these men had a particular way that the purpose of God was to be effected through their gifts, calling, positions, and even personality to touch and transform the world around them. It is the same for me.

Father, may I not be negligent of Your purposes to which I am called to carry in my generation. What are the gifts, calling, and specific course I am to run today as a carrier of Your purpose?

DAY 14

I AM A CHILD OF GOD

But as many as received Him, to them He gave the right to become children of God to those who believe in His name. (Jn. 1:12 NKJV)

To be a child of God means to have received Jesus. To receive someone is to extend an open heart to who that person is. It is to accept what they bring to my life. It is place of trust. To open my heart to Jesus is to accept the fellowship of His life with mine and mine with His. It is not about "adding" Jesus to my list of beliefs, but is the experience of giving my life to be absorbed into His and His into mine. It is to accept all that He brings me from the Father, and what He brings me is the right and power to be a child of Light, a child of Love and Truth, and who now has Abba's fathering and purposeful involvement in my life.

Before, I had no power to walk in the Light. I was lost in darkness and lies, unable to save myself or know God. In receiving Jesus, I am brought into Hashem's family. He is my Father, Jesus is my Brother, and Holy Spirit is my Comforter and Teacher. I am no longer wandering around trying to find comfort or where I fit in life. I know who I am and who I belong to. I have a family identity.

Abba, thank You for making me a part of Your holy family and that I am no longer alone or without a place to call home. Show me today who else needs Your fathering care.

DAY 15

I AM A CITY BUILDER

They will rebuild the ancient ruins, repairing cities destroyed long ago. They will revive them, though they have been deserted for many generations. (Isa. 61:4 NLT)

My Heavenly Father is a builder. He cares about people, cities, and nations. He calls me to work with Him in rebuilding what has been ruined and destroyed by the works of darkness. As a believer, I co-labor with Jesus in the Father's passion to repair communities so that they thrive in love, peace, and the destiny He intends for them.

Cities and nations, like people, have a divine destiny to know God's glory and to flourish in it. To flourish they need heaven's rain to water them, pillars of wisdom to support them, teachers of truth to feed them, and hands of love to help them. No place is too ruined that His grace cannot rebuild the lives and hearts there. To the contrary, the deeper the darkness the greater the need for Hashem's sons and daughters to come and build and repair what has been ruined, so that life may fill the streets again. I am called to build with God.

Abba, thank You for the opportunity to build with You in my community and nation. How do You want me to show up and build with You today?

DAY 16
I AM A CONDUIT OF LIVING WATER

He who believes in Me, as the Scripture said, "From his innermost being will flow rivers of living water." (John 7:38 NASB)

A conduit is a channel that facilitates the movement of something, such as water or energy. As Christ's body, I am a conduit of the movement and power of God in the Earth! As Christ's life pours into me, I, in turn, become a conduit of His life to others. He does not call me a stagnant pool, but a channel of His living river — a movement of divine power to bring healing, restoration, and growth to individuals, families, and regions.

The more I receive of Jesus, the greater the flow of His life through me. There are souls all around me that are dry, thirsting and longing for heavenly waters to restore their spirit with life. My intimacy with Christ and Holy Spirit make a difference to the world around me and whether it remains dry and barren or blooms with life.

As a believer, I have a responsibility to be a conduit of Christ and to put away foolish things that act as river-stoppers and water-drainers in my life, such as prayerlessness, endless entertainments, and sin. I need water to live and so does this world.

Lord, may I drink from You richly today. Remove anything that is stopping up my receiving from You and Your flow through me. Who do You want to water through me today?

DAY 17
I AM A CROWN IN THE LORD'S HAND

You will be a crown of splendor in the Lord 's hand, a royal diadem in the hand of your God. (Isa. 62:3 NIV)

A crown is a symbol of authority, dignity, and power. It is a symbol of victory. Hashem sees me as His crown, a golden trophy of His love and grace. The work of Christ and the power of His blood fashions me with dignity, authority, and victory. Father holds me in His hand as a symbol of His triumph over all that the enemy has tried to do in my life. He holds me as a jeweled crown declaring my position of authority in Him. His face beams with pleasure as He holds me in His hand and places me where He desires for the purpose of releasing His Kingdom authority and victory. I am not a loser hidden in a corner; He is making me a victor in every way and He loves to display that.

Father, thank You for every triumph in my life; it is a radiant display of Your goodness. Where do you want me to shine with Your Kingdom authority today?

DAY 18

I AM CALLED OF GOD

But to those called by God to salvation, both Jews and Gentiles, Christ is the power of God and the wisdom of God. (1 Cor. 1:24 NLT)

To be called is to be invited to something special. I am invited by God to an abundant and eternal life of power and wisdom in Christ. And that is pretty special. I am not the kid who doesn't get picked…I've been picked by God Himself! I have a personal invitation to know life in place of death, healing instead of sickness, and freedom instead of bondage. The divine hand has delivered a personal note through Jesus inviting me to come and experience His love, presence, and power in place of my powerless living.

I have been invited to receive divine wisdom and counsel in place of confusion and chaos. I have an invitation to come out of darkness and into the Light and fulfill the purpose for which I have been created. Such an invitation is priceless…and it has been given to whosoever will receive it.

Abba Father, thank You for Your invitation that was sealed and delivered by the blood of Jesus. Teach me to fully show up in answer to Your call. Who do You want me to share with today about Your letter of invitation to them?

DAY 19

I AM CHANGED BY DIVINE KINDNESS

Don't you see how wonderfully kind, tolerant, and patient God is with you? Does this mean nothing to you? Can't you see that His kindness is intended to turn you from your sin? (Rom. 2:4 NLT)

Fear of punishment from an angry parent may catch the attention of an unruly child to bring momentary change. But lasting change is the result of the heart becoming tender and pliable through love and kindness. God says that His tender mercies create inward transformation as His gentleness brings my heart to humble repentance. God is a just God and He is also kind.

It is God's infinite grace, not anger, that draws me to Himself. His love makes me want to change. His lovingkindness makes my hand loose its grasp on sin and self in order to reach out to God's own hand extended to me in love. His patience with me teaches me to also be patient. He is so beautiful in His kindness that it makes me want to be kind, too.

Abba, thank You that You are not mad at me and You don't use anger to correct me. You hate darkness and grieve at my agreement with it, but even when I was lost in sin it was Your kindness that drew me to You. Thank You for continuing to change me with Your generosity. How do You want me to show Your kindness and generous love to others today?

DAY 20
I AM CHOSEN FOR A HOLY LIFE

According as He hath chosen us in Him before the foundation of the world, that we should be holy and without blame before Him in love.
(Eph. 1:4 KJV)

Holiness means to be set apart for God, to be free from anything that would corrupt my ability to walk with Him. The Spirit of holiness is divine life and power to rise from death — spiritually, emotionally, mentally, idealogically; it is power to break free from anything that contains me and hinders the flow of God's life in me. I am chosen for such a life.

Before creation God chose me to be His, to be a life immersed in His love and washed from all blame. He chose me for a life of power. He selected me to be completely His in spirit, soul, and body, and to be empowered by His Spirit for grand purposes. He saw me and He wanted me! He established the cross and resurrection of Christ to be the door to glory and a holy life where I can think holy thoughts, walk in a blameless way, and advance triumphantly in holy purposes.

Holiness is not about the way I do my hair or the clothes I wear, but is the sanctifying presence of the Holy Spirit to free me from all that defiles and disempowers me as Hashem's child. I want to be holy. I want to be like my Father. I want to be free from anything obstructing a life of Kingdom purpose with power.

Father, thank You for choosing me for a life separated unto You. Is there anything unclean and hindering my life that keeps me from You and Your desires for me that needs to be removed today?

DAY 21

I AM CHRIST'S BRIDE

For the husband is the head of the wife as Christ is the head of the church, His body, of which He is the Savior. (Eph. 5:23 NIV)

As a believer, I am a part of Jesus' Body…His Bride. The "Bride" is a metaphor for those in covenant with God. The Bride is not a physical building where a service is attended, but is the corporate heart of all who love Yeshua as their first Love and have committed their lives to Him. The Heavenly Bridegroom (Yeshua) has given His life, now the Bride gives Him her life in return because of love.

I am Yeshua's covenant beloved. He empowers me for a life of victory. He lifted me from death and has seated me beside Him as a royal bride. He cherishes me as a Heavenly Husband and makes me fruitful in every way. He puts a crown on my head and adorns me with the riches of His grace. He listens to me and speaks comforting words when I am hurting, and rejoices with me when I am delighted. He never harms me. We share intimate fellowship in an abiding commitment through thick and thin, in sickness and in health, and in good times and in difficulties. We do not forsake one another.

This covenant bond is a selfless sharing of my life with Him. He is my first Love. I keep myself pure and live my life as being one with Him — one with His heart, His thoughts, and His works. I am not a silenced, battered, or subjugated bride; I am a royal bride with ruling authority carrying His name.

Yeshua, thank You for the joy of being a part of this radiant company that loves You. Deepen the bond of my heart with Yours today. Teach me how to be more one with You in heart, mind, and thoughts as a bride with a bridegroom.

DAY 22

I AM CLOTHED WITH COMPASSION

As God's chosen people, holy and dearly loved, clothe yourselves with compassion, kindness, humility, gentleness, and patience.
(Col. 3:12 NIV)

My Heavenly Father is compassionate; He is merciful. To be merciful is to withhold punishment or harsh treatment when it is in your power to do so. As His dearly loved child I lean on His heart and I learn to be as He is — kind, gentle, patient and full of mercy. This is how He is with me, so this is how I am to be with others.

To be clothed means that I pick up a garment and put it on. In some things God Himself comes and clothes me with a garment, such as with His love or authority. Other times I have to put a garment on myself, such as compassion, mercy, gentleness, and patience. I am to show up in life dressed as His compassionate child. I don't turn my head away from someone in need. I don't ignore another's difficulty and say, "It's not my concern," or "I don't get involved." I don't treat others harshly when it is in my power to do so. I don't punish people with my bad attitudes and actions.

Compassion is part of what characterizes or identifies me as my Father's son or daughter, just as a crown identifies a king.

Abba, where do I need to put on mercy and compassion toward others today? Where do You want me to withhold harshness and be kindly involved?

DAY 23

I AM CONFIDENT IN GOD

So let us come boldly to the throne of our gracious God. There we will receive His mercy, and we will find grace to help us when we need it most... This is the confidence we have in approaching God: that if we ask anything according to His will, He hears us.
(Heb. 4:16 NLT; 1 John 5:14 NIV)

As a believer, the way of grace to come confidently and without fear to God's throne is open before me. There I will receive help for whatever I need. He promises that whatever I ask in line with His will, He will grant it to me. As the Loving, Merciful, and Just Judge, His will is to prosper me in every way because of the blood of His Son.

As I look to Him for help on that basis, He says He will not deny my requests in His courts. The blood of Jesus gives me legal right to the ear of God, and thus confidence that He receives me and grants me my requests. I am not an outcast before His throne.

It is His will that I be made whole, be healed, be delivered, and be safe. It is His will that I receive all that Yeshua purchased for me on the cross. It is His will that I succeed in life and purpose.

Abba, thank You for the certainty in times of need that You care and answer my cries. Thank You for being a Just and True King. What do You want me to come confidently to You about today and find help in my time of need?

DAY 24
I AM CREATED FOR DOMINION

God blessed them; and God said to them, "Be fruitful and multiply, and fill the Earth, and subdue it; and rule over the fish of the sea and over the birds of the sky and over every living thing that moves on the earth."
(Gen. 1:28 NASB)

When Elohim, Creator and Ruler of the Universe, formed man and woman in His image, He created them to rule over the works of His hands. Ps. 115:16 says that the heavens of the heavens are the Lord's, but He has given the earth to mankind to rule. This ruling includes everything that concerns land, sea, air — all that fills it and influences what takes place there.

As a redeemed child of God, I am brought back to original design; I am the head and not the tail. I am a ruler and not a slave. I have a charge from Hashem to govern Earth with Him and prosper it in the way He intends. It means protecting territories from evil, as well as caring for land and society in every way. It means showing up in my family and community, showing up in prayer and taking practical actions to prosper lives. As I pray, Hashem will show me specific ways I am to govern, whether through impact in the realm of family, education, the arts, business, or in civil duties. As I talk with Him, He will give me counsel for His Kingdom work in my sphere of influence.

Father, where do I need to take practical action for my territory today?

DAY 25

I AM CREATED FOR GOOD THINGS

For we are God's masterpiece. He has created us anew in Christ Jesus, so we can do the good things He planned for us long ago.
(Eph. 2:10 NLT)

I am a masterpiece of God's handiwork that He created for good things. I am a high-quality, first-rate design fashioned for excellent things. A masterpiece refers to a genius piece of artwork. The God of Glory only makes genius works of art, including me! I am not a piece of junk. I am not a random accident of creation. I am a brilliantly designed and detailed vessel in the Potter's hand. I am a remarkable painting of the Artist's inspired vision. As a believer, I am a rare and priceless instrument in the hands of the Master.

My life, talents, gifts, and even personality are chosen and given me from Him to reveal Him to this world. These are given for me to do excellent things in life. He wants me to use them to bless the world I live in. I am to be to this world as God's golden vessel of service to pour out divine blessings. The work of Christ polishes me as an instrument for releasing the sound of Heaven on Earth…a sound that heals, renews, and restores.

Abba, thank You for taking such exquisite care in designing me. Show me what excellent and good things You want to do through me today as Your masterpiece.

DAY 26

I AM CREATIVE

Then God said, "Let Us make man in Our image, according to Our likeness." (Gen. 1:26 NASB)

I was made in the likeness of the Creator. Thus, I am creative. I cannot create from what does not exist like He can, but I can create something new, something not yet seen in this world, from the materials He made and the ideas He gives me. The ideas for products, goods, and inventions are infinite! Inspired products and goods are meant to be a blessing to many.

Creativity can be expressed in myriad ways, not just in products and goods, but in song, music, painting, writing as well as administration. A good administrator or organizer can design functional order for advancing businesses, taking disorder and making new processes with new strategies. In Zechariah 1, the creative ones (craftsmen) were said to play an important part in overthrowing the destructive power of the enemy. Divine creativity is a weapon in God's hands to throw down the works of darkness.

Abba Father, thank You for making me like You. Show me today how Your creativity wants to be expressed through me for bringing something good to this world and for destroying evil works.

DAY 27
I AM CRUCIFIED WITH CHRIST

I have been crucified with Christ; and it is no longer I who live, but Christ lives in me; and the life which I now live in the flesh I live by faith in the Son of God, who loved me and gave Himself up for me. (Gal. 2:20 NASB)

To be crucified with Christ means that my old life hangs on the cross with Jesus. It is dead. It is over. It is finished. The old sinful life is buried with all its passions and lusts and rebellion against Elohim. I now live with Christ in me, filling my days with fellowship and purposeful living for the Father's desires.

I used to trust in myself, following my own ideas, my own wisdom, and my own way of doing things, but now I put all my trust in Jesus, following Him, and walking in the life He has for me. He gave Himself for me, now I give myself for Him. I commit my way to His leading.

Jesus, thank You for your life given for me that I might have a new life in you. Show me today any place where I may be living by a dead pattern that has no part in this new life. May Your resurrection life fill me and flow out to touch others.

DAY 28
I AM A DWELLER IN GOD'S LOVE

If you keep My commandments, you will abide in My love, just as I have kept My Father's commandments and abide in His love. (John 15:10 ESV)

Hashem's commandments are an evidence of His love for me. He loves me enough to give me life-giving charges as a good Father to a son or daughter. These empower me for success, prosperity, and well-being. Keeping His words is an evidence of my love for Him. I treasure what He says because I love Him. As I obey Him, I experience His love because all His commands and words spring from His love. Love is the very sum of His words and so can only be guarded in my heart through love and not by religious law. I cannot keep His charges in my own fleshly strength either, so I keep close to the Holy Spirit and ask Him to fill me continually with love, a love that treasures Father's charges to me.

Jesus kept His Father's words because He loved Him, and He never moved outside the divine engagement of that love.

Father, thank You for Your commands that are an evidence of Your love for me. Where do I need to walk in greater love for You today regarding what You have told me?

DAY 29

I AM DEARLY LOVED

As God's chosen people, holy and dearly loved… (Col. 3:12 NIV)

I am dearly loved by God. Dearly means greatly, extremely, exceedingly! He looks at me with great passion. I am the apple of His eye and the center of His affections. I am an adored child to a proud Father, and a precious bride to an adoring Bridegroom. This understanding is not an arrogant idea about who I am, but a righteous knowledge that drives away self-demeaning and self-destructive mindsets derived from something other than God's Word. I will never succeed in divine purpose as long as I adhere to dark ideologies based on lies that work to sabotage how I think about God's love and plan for me. His love is the foundation and fountain of my life and purpose. I am not unloved.

God's deep love for me never changes, and it never will. It is extreme in its measure, exceeding in its perfection. It is constant and unwavering. It runs deep like the currents of the sea, ever sustaining my life no matter what I may be experiencing in circumstances or other relationships. His love is great and being dearly loved by Him gives me buoyancy when the sea of life gets rough. Because of His enduring love I will not sink, for He watches over me and holds my hand in His.

Father, thank You for dearly loving me. Show me any place in my thoughts that tells me differently, for it is a lie sent from the enemy. I am dear to You, and so are those all around me dear to You.

DAY 30
I AM AN EFFECTUAL DOER OF GOD'S WORD

But one who looks intently at the perfect law, the law of liberty, and
abides by it, not having become a forgetful hearer but an effectual doer,
this man will be blessed in what he does. (James 1:25 NASB)

To be an effectual doer means to read God's Word and do it! It is to
daily look into His Word of truth and connect with Him in prayer,
thought, and intentional action about what I hear and see from Him in
His words. It means not ignoring or forgetting what I read, what He
quickened to my heart and mind, and what I heard Him say to my spirit
man. In doing so, I am promised to be blessed in what I do for when I fill
myself with Him, then what I do will reflect Him and be from Him. As I
dwell in God's truth and engage His words, He will bless that
engagement with His presence, guidance, and power.

Father, thank You for Your Truth that sets me free to give intentional
actions to Your Word. I do not want to be lazy and forgetful. Show me
any place where my listening needs to shift from passivity to full
attention with action.

DAY 31
I AM AN ENCOURAGER

Strengthen the weak hands, and make firm the feeble knees.
Say to those who are fearful-hearted, "Be strong, do not fear! Behold,
your God will come with vengeance, with the recompense of God;
He will come and save you." (Isa. 35:3-4 NKJV)

God calls me to strengthen myself in Him, to break free of fear and
look to Him…for He is coming to me now! I am to renew my mind and
focus my heart on the truth that He is able to do above and beyond what I
could ask or think. He wants me to encourage others to do the same.

God has a good plan for my life. He wants me to advance in His rich
purposes and not be stuck in the past, weighted with sin, disabled with
fear, or entangled by the cares of this world. He also doesn't want me to
be discouraged. He knows the difficulties I face, and what others face,
too. He wants me to rise and shine in His love, and to use my voice to
strengthen another's faith in Him, as well.

There is nothing more encouraging than to receive hopeful words
from someone who has walked through a similar difficulty and come out
the other side. Father wants me to have an altruistic mindset; to help

others move forward in life and divine purpose, just as He has sent others to help me move forward. He says I am to remind others that He hears their prayers and is on the way with His saving power. He is at work on their behalf just as He is at work on my behalf; He wants me to remind them of that.

Abba, who do You want to encourage through me today? Who needs to hear that You are coming to help them?!

DAY 32
I AM EMPOWERED BY GRACE

> For by grace you have been saved through faith; and that not of yourselves, it is the gift of God. (Eph. 2:8 NASB)

Grace is a gift from God. It is not an excuse for me to sin; it is not the divine eye deliberately overlooking my wrongdoings. Rather, it is divine power for a transformed life. Grace is the divine influence of the Holy Spirit upon my heart for effecting inward change, ever conforming me to the image of Christ. Grace is the power of God that shifts my thoughts and motives and endues me with an ability to move with God in a way I once could not.

Grace is the presence of God that draws me close to Him; it softens my heart to His work and transforming touch on my life. Grace awakens the affections of my heart towards God, and empowers me to experience intimate fellowship with Him. Grace is the priceless present given me through the cross and resurrection of Jesus. It is a gift that empowers me to actively follow Him out of darkness and into the Light. Grace is the heavenly gift of the Spirit that enables me to walk on Earth with Heaven in my spirit.

Father, thank You for the gift of grace, for the presence and influence of the Holy Spirit to conform me to the image of Your Son.

DAY 33
I AM EMPOWERED BY THE HOLY SPIRIT

> But you will receive power when the Holy Spirit comes upon you. And you will be my witnesses, telling people about me everywhere—in Jerusalem, throughout Judea, in Samaria, and to the ends of the earth. (Acts 1:8 NLT)

The person of the Holy Spirit comes to empower me with divine ability for a divine work on Earth. The word power (Grk. "dunamis") refers to a strength, ability, and miracle performing power from God. It is divine power that breaks through suddenly with divine action to effect supernatural change in a natural world. Dunamis is where we get our English word dynamite!

Jesus told His disciples to wait for the Holy Spirit whom He would send and that He would give them power to do the work they were to do. 500 were told to wait for this power; 120 chose to do so. And when Holy Spirit came, He baptized the 120 with fire and dunamis! They burst with boldness, moved past personal abilities, and thousands were saved in a day.

Miracles, healings, and deliverances became common place as the Holy Spirit moved through the apostles in dynamite power to break the works of darkness holding regions. This same power of God is given to me today. The Holy Spirit still wants to move with power to free people and restore them to the God-given life He designed for them. He wants to move through me with an ability that is beyond my own to effect supernatural change in a natural world. He empowers me for a purpose.

Jesus, fill me now with the Holy Spirit and fire! Release dunamis in me with boldness to advance Your Kingdom that brings breakthrough to lives and regions!

DAY 34

I AM EMPOWERED TO MAKE WEALTH

But you shall remember the Lord your God, for it is He who is giving you power to make wealth, that He may confirm His covenant which He swore to your fathers, as it is this day. (Deut. 8:18 NASB)

Wealth is the means by which one sustains life, advances in purpose, and increases influence. Wealth is strength. It is a means by which good can be done for others. The ability to make wealth is a blessing and ability that comes from God. Prospering is a part of being in covenant with Him, as His Word states; poverty is not a part of covenant blessing. When wealth increases, God wants me to remember that He is the source of my wealth. He wants me to use finances wisely for Him as a good steward of His blessings that come through covenant with Him; including faithful giving to Him and Kingdom purposes through tithes and offerings.

Power to make wealth is given me to help others. God loves people and wants me to be able to do good for others through the power of blessed abilities and increase that I receive from Him. As I seek His face and get His counsel, He will give me understanding and wisdom to make wealth and what to do with it.

Father, thank You that You care about every detail of my life, including my finances. Thank You for giving me creative ideas, innovative inventions, and divine connections for helping my finances grow and to have power to bless. How do You want me to increase wealth today? Where do You want me to give?

DAY 35

I AM EMPOWERED TO PROFIT

Thus says the Lord, your Redeemer, the Holy One of Israel,
"I am the Lord your God who teaches you to profit, who leads you in the way you should go." (Isa. 48:17 NASB)

My Father loves me and wants me to succeed in life, and so He teaches me how to profit. To profit means to excel and be useful. It is to excel in abilities and insight that fit me for a higher place of usefulness. The word profit also means to ascend a mountain, to rise above as a noble or prince — as one who rules rather than as one who is subjugated, as being the head and not the tail.

To profit also means to stand on a summit. A summit is a high place, a peak where I can see long distances, new horizons, and what could not be seen before. A summit gives me clarity and new perspective. Clarity and perspective are critical keys to excelling in anything. Clouded thinking and limited perspectives can keep me stuck, blocked, and frustrated.

God says that as part of His redemption in my life He trains me to ascend from where I am, to see in new ways, and to excel as He leads me in the direction that I am to go, marching victoriously in excelled use and influence. This is who He is with me as the Holy One, my Lord and God.

Being on the summit is to be in His presence above the shadows and ceilings of limitation. On the summit, I get His directives, receive His wisdom, grasp His inspiration, and learn His timing. As I get these new perspectives for excelling on my journey, He also instructs me to commit my thoughts, plans, labors, and endeavors to Him. As I entrust my way to Him, He says that my thoughts and plans will be established — they will be securely determined, rightly directed, provided for, and accomplished (Prov. 16:3). And so I will profit and excel.

Holy One, You have created me to be a noble one; not an unprofitable servant. Where do You want me to rise above circumstances today and see in a new way that will profit me for excelling in Kingdom usefulness? Teach me today, Lord, how to ascend in You and see something new, with strategy to excel!

DAY 36
I AM THE EARTH'S CARETAKER

Then the Lord God took the man and put him into the garden of
Eden to cultivate it and keep it. (Gen. 2:15 NASB)

Hashem is so very purposeful in all that He does. He loves me and He loves this world. He has placed me here to take care of it and everything about it — land, nature, people, and society. I am here for such a time as this. As His child He puts me in a place (home, work, community, and nation) where He walks with me and charges me to take care of that place with Him. I cannot take care of the entire world, but I can seek how to participate with God in guarding and prospering the area where He puts me. This includes all that concerns that place physically, spiritually, intellectually, emotionally. He may even call me to participate with Him about a distant land where I do not reside.

My years on Earth have an important purpose in this matter. Knowing how to accomplish this work comes through walking intimately with Him. My voice, talents, and gifts are the tools He gives me for my work as Earth's anointed caretaker. The Holy Spirit teaches me, and His anointing empowers me, for releasing Heaven into my territory, and prospering it with supernatural life in a natural world.

Father, show me today how to take care of my place, and what all that entails. Teach me how to protect the land and its inhabitants through prayer, and to prosper it through Your love, truth, and presence.

DAY 37
I AM A FAITHFUL STEWARD

Moreover, it is required of stewards that one be found faithful.
(1 Cor. 4:2 NKJV)

A steward is someone who manages another's affairs. A faithful steward is one who is trustworthy, dependable, and loyal in taking care of those affairs. A steward is to be thoughtful and responsible in caring for what has been given him with the view of causing them to prosper for the master or owner. He understands that he is accountable to the one whose affairs he is entrusted with. An unfaithful steward is one who is lazy, unreliable, or even deceitful regarding what matters to the master.

I am a steward of all that Adonai has given me, from personal care to household affairs to finances to civil duties. I represent His true ownership in all these matters. I am accountable for my mind, body, spirit, education, time, gifts, and involvement in the relationships and responsibilities that Adonai has given me. I am to steward the revelations He gives me, the words He speaks to me, the experiences He gives me, and the learning I've received from Him on my journey.

Lord, help me to be diligent in faithfully caring for what You have given me. Where do I need to be more reliable and dependable in how I show up in relationships and responsibilities, and regarding some revelation I've received from You?

DAY 38

I AM A FOLLOWER OF THE SHEPHERD

My sheep listen to my voice; I know them,
and they follow me. (John 10:27 NLT)

Jesus is my Shepherd and life-guide. He shows me the journey God has planned for me. He talks to me about the plans of the Father. Everyone who is born of God has the capacity to hear the Father, the Son, and the Holy Spirit. Sometimes I think I can't hear God, but then I discover that His talking comes in many different ways — through Scripture, His voice in my spirit man, inspired thoughts, or an insight. He also uses dreams, other people, angels, even a movie. He is not limited in how He speaks to me.

Or it may be that He is sitting peacefully beside me and wants me to be quiet and still myself until He makes His thoughts clear to me. I've learned that He is never in as much of a hurry with things as I am!

Jesus said that His sheep listen to Him and follow Him. Listening is an art, especially for the human nature that loves to do its own thing without listening. Listening must be practiced. Things like distractions, self-centeredness, anxiety, passive listening, and judgments against God all hinder good listening. If I am to hear Him clearly and follow Him closely, I must humbly give Him my full attention to what He is saying, consider His words, and ask how He wants me to take action.

Being a follower of the Shepherd means to accompany Him through quiet places, beautiful places, and even places that are challenging. Yet even when I go through the valley of the shadow of death, He is there waiting, setting a table before me in the presence of my enemies. He who leads me to, will also lead me through.

Jesus, thank You for being my Shepherd, ever leading me into greater realms of life and light. Every place you lead me to and through is designed with my good in mind. How can I be a better listener to You today?

DAY 39

I AM A FOLLOWER OF THE WAY-MAKER

The one who breaks open will come up before them; they will break out, pass through the gate and go out by it; their king will pass before them, with the Lord at their head. (Micah 2:13 NIV)

Life is full of difficulties and challenges — mountains of impossibility, impassable roads, and obstacles that hinder my way. I may not know how to get through, get over, or get around them, but God does! Jesus promises to go before me and to break open the way for me. He is the Anointed One for breakthrough! He also gives me insight and authority to overcome the obstacles that work to stop me. I may not see instant victory, but breakthrough is mine as I walk with the Way-Maker.

Jesus, thank You for going before me, no matter what my eyes currently see. You are there ahead of me making a way for me where there seems to be no way. You send Your angels ahead of me, too, as they work to help advance my way in Father's assignments. Where do You want me to believe You for breakthrough today?

DAY 40

I AM FASHIONED FOR GOD'S GLORY

Even every one that is called by My name: for I have created him for My glory, I have formed him; yea, I have made him. (Isa. 43:7 KJV)

God's glory is the radiant splendor of all who He is. Moses said, "Show me Your ways, teach me Your paths, show me Your glory." In response, God showed Moses His forgiveness, goodness, compassion, and lovingkindness.

As a human being fashioned by God in His likeness, He designed me with a special capacity to know Him and experience His glory in a way that all the rest of His created works cannot. Even the angels will never know what it feels like to experience divine forgiveness or compassion in the midst of brokenness. I have a capacity to know God and experience His radiance in my spirit and soul in a beautiful and glorious way.

Jesus activates that capacity in me to bring me into a vibrant reality in God and His healing mercies, cleansing power, and restorative compassions. The presence of Jesus is the gateway to the beautiful realm of God's glory. I was made for such a life — to know His glory and to glorify Him.

Father, show me Your ways, teach me Your paths, and show me Your glory today. What splendor do You want to show me today?

DAY 41
I AM FAVORED FOR STRENGTH

For You are the glory of their strength, and in Your favor our
horn is exalted. (Ps. 89:17 NKJV)

True success and strength in life does not come by my own power and might, but by God who is my strength. God's presence is the source of all my strength for every part of life, and what's more is that He gives me favor me in order to give me power. He turns His face towards me and extends His scepter to me to assign me might where I have none. His acceptance of me is an energizing force that flows from Him and into me. He royally decrees my victory through the blood of Jesus and enables me to overcome every enemy and obstacle that I might succeed in the purpose to which I am called. God is not only with me, but He is also for me. It delights Him to be my strength and support.

Father, thank You for Your favor that strengthens my soul for whatever this day brings. You will not fail, Lord, so I will not fail because I am in You and You are in me, and You support me strongly.

DAY 42
I AM FILLED WITH THE HOLY SPIRIT

And they were all filled with the Holy Spirit and began to speak with
other tongues, as the Spirit gave them utterance. (Acts 2:4 NKJV)

To be filled means to be full of something, or in this case Someone. When Jesus' disciples were filled with the Holy Spirit it was a fulfillment of a promise from the Father that they would be a people not only born of Him, but filled with His Spirit for walking in divine purpose with power.

God created us to be a holy people filled with Himself for relationship and divine purpose. I can fill myself with many things — things of the world or even religious things — but I am not called to be full of the world or religion but with the Spirit of God. And when the Spirit comes, everything comes alive and is new — new power, new vision, new abilities. Even my language becomes new as the Holy Spirit speaks to the Father through me in His own language of intercession. I may not understand the language of the Spirit, but the Father understands and I experience His quickening power in my spirit man.

Father wants me to have His promise of being filled with His Spirit. If I am not filled with Him, I will surely be filled with something else for the human life is designed to be filled. John spoke of the Holy Spirit, Jesus spoke of Him, too, and when Holy Spirit came at Pentecost the disciples received Him. They received Him, were filled, and their lives were transformed into Kingdom revolutionaries.

Father, I want my life filled and revolutionized by Your Holy Spirit! I want all that You have for me. Fill me with Your Spirit today!

DAY 43

I AM FORGIVEN

Blessed are those whose lawless deeds are forgiven and whose sins are covered. (Rom. 4:7 ESV)

To be forgiven is to have my lawless past wiped clean by Yeshua's blood. I now stand in God's presence legally absolved of guilt and debt for wrong doing. The charges have all been dismissed! I am released from a dark prison of broken divine laws that would have sent me on to an eternal damnation apart from God. Jesus has taken my punishment not only for me but as me on the cross. I am not left in the prison of condemnation.

The gavel of justice resounds in the courts of Heaven. I am forgiven! There is no more condemnation, no accusation, no weight of sin and its shameful guilt to hold me captive. I could do nothing on my own to remove my guilt, nor did I do anything to deserve such grace. I simply came to Jesus to receive His offer — a divine exchange of my guilt for God's forgiveness because of the cross. The weight of sin is off my shoulders and I can breathe the breath of heaven!

The Judge of Heaven then turns to me and says, "You have been forgiven your crimes, now go and forgive those who have sinned against you."

Yeshua, thank You for standing in my place and taking my sin on the cross so that today I have the joy of living an abundant life rather than in a place of darkness, condemned to an eternity separated from God. I now lift my face unashamed. Show me who I need to forgive today. Show me also who needs to receive Your forgiveness in order to breathe heaven's atmosphere, too.

DAY 44

I AM FREE

So if the Son makes you free, you will be free indeed.
(John 8:36 NASB)

I am not only forgiven for my sins, but I am free from sin's dominion in my life. The power of Yeshua's blood has broken the chains that I could not break on my own. Bondage is no longer my identity, freedom is. I am free from captivity in my spirit and in my mind. I am free from addictions and strongholds. I am free to worship God with all my heart, soul, mind, and strength — these were once in captivity but now are free! I am free to walk in divine purpose with strength and power. I am free from the fear of man, the pain of the past and any fear of my future. I am free to reach up and receive from God, and move forward in all He has for me.

Thank You, Jesus, for making me free from the power of sin and death. Thank You for freedom from the carnal mind and ungodliness. Show me any place where I may still be holding on to a pattern of bondage in my soul so that I can bring it to You and break its hold. You want me to be fully free.

DAY 45

I AM FULL OF HOPE

Be strong and let your heart take courage,
all you who hope in the LORD! (Ps. 31:24 NASB)

Hope is more than wishful thinking. It is an expectation of good that I may not yet see manifest, but it is coming! Life can be full of hurts and disappointments, but I can be encouraged in this truth that God will not fail me. My life is in His hands...all of it. And so my expectation of good is in Him and His unceasing goodness towards me. He is my source of good things coming my way. Things may look dark at the moment, but the light of dawn is on its way for He has promised to help me. He is for me. He does not lie.

I am not hopeless; I have an expectancy from God. His promises are true and not false. I wait on Him and I lean on His strength. He will bring things to pass for me. So I take courage because my life is in Him and He is greater than the things of this world or my abilities to make something happen. He will order my steps and command His goodness to overtake me.

Abba Father, thank You that I can expect good things from You who loves me dearly. Show me any place where hopelessness is battering my mind and faith. Let it now be replaced with trust and expectation in You.

DAY 46

I AM FRUITFUL

God blessed them; and God said to them, "Be fruitful and multiply, and fill the Earth, and subdue it; and rule over the fish of the sea and over the birds of the sky and over every living thing that moves on the earth."
(Gen. 1:28 NASB)

Fruitfulness happens when a seed is planted and nurtured. As it grows and matures fruit is produced. Multiplication happens when that same process is repeated with the seed of the fruit, producing multiplied new fruit.

Hashem has placed within me the ability to be fruitful and to multiply in infinite ways. There are seeds inside me waiting to be developed and matured — seeds of thought and creativity, physical seeds, intellectual seeds, seeds of relationships, business ideas, ministry callings, and personal talents. Every word of Scripture I've heard or read is a seed waiting to be planted and nurtured in the soil of my heart. All these have a harvest to manifest as I nurture them with intentional action.

God gives me the seed I am to cultivate, whether physical, spiritual, or intellectual, until it bears fruit. Jesus said that fruit glorifies the Father; it also benefits others. My fruitfulness is meant to bless Hashem and enrich those around me.

Abba, help me to see the seeds in my life that need watering and nurturing until they are fully developed and fruitful, whether it is be with child, a calling, or a creative idea.

43

DAY 47

I AM A GENERATIONAL ENCOURAGER

God also said to Moses, "Say this to the people of Israel: Yahweh, the God of your ancestors — the God of Abraham, the God of Isaac, and the God of Jacob — has sent me to you. This is My eternal name, My name to remember for all generations." (Ex. 3:15 NLT)

Here Yahweh links His personal identity to His Name that connects the generations. He is a covenant God from generation to generation. And so He commands me to remind the next generation of all that He has done in my life and in the lives of those before me — to talk about His power and involvement in my life, and how He showed up big for me when everything seemed impossible. He came and did what I could not do for myself.

Hashem charges me to tell the next generation about His unfailing love and goodness, to tell them about His covenant through Yeshua, and the vow to care for them through Christ. I am to tell them about His faithfulness in doing what He says He will do. As an older person to a younger person I may have different tastes, but they long to hear wisdom and stories of God's love. They want to know the victories of His deliverances and hope in impossible situations.

Hashem wants the generations united together in a powerful revelation of who He is with us as His people. As a Father, He loves unity and who we are in Him. And there is no better way to cultivate the power of identity and unity of the generations than to rehearse the testimony of God and the greatness of who He is with us as His people.

Abba, who do You want me to share with today, especially in my family, about the great things You have done for me? Let me rehearse the glory of who You are, whether in person or on paper. I pray for wisdom and that my words will inspire their heart to believe and trust in You.

DAY 48

I AM A GIFT

Children are a gift from the Lord; they are a reward from Him.
(Ps. 127:3 NLT)

The word gift means a blessing and heritage. The very fact that I am born on Earth means that I am a gift and a heritage to my earthly parents,

44

whether it seemed so or not. Whatever my relationship with them was or wasn't, God still calls me a gift and a heritage from Him. I am not an accident. I am a reward of His lovingkindness. He wanted me to come into existence, to have life on this earth as a gift from Him.

As Abba's child, I am also a gift and a reward for Him. I am a heritage for Him. The love, honor, and relationship I give Him is a gift to Him and a rich return for all the love and care He gives me. As God's child, I am also a purposeful gift from Him to this world. He raises me and sends me into the world to reveal Him and His goodness, and to bring Him glory.

Abba, how can I show You more love today for bringing me into this world as Your rich reward? How can I be a rich gift to my earthly parents or those who have nurtured and helped me grow in life? Teach me to be a blessing to them through my prayers and actions.

DAY 49

I AM A GIFTED CHILD

For God's gifts and His call can never be withdrawn...To each is given
the manifestation of the Spirit for the common good.
(Rom. 11:29 ESV; 1 Cor. 12:7 ESV)

Hashem loves to give gifts! He made me to not only be a gift to my parents and Himself, but He gives me special gifts to be a blessing to others. Gifts are special abilities for doing something. Gifts are never about me, but about what God wants to do through me. Every gift is a manifestation of His Spirit in me that He wants to use to bring a special supply of His goodness to others. They are ways that His Spirit wants to manifest through me for revealing God and glorifying Him in the Earth. They are not given to glorify me.

Romans 12, 1 Corinthians 12, and Ephesians 4 tell about different gifts that God gives to different people. He is the One who chooses what gift goes to whom. God gives me gifts designed to work with the rest of Yeshua's Body. Together we function as a complete Body.

I am a needed part of Christ's Body for demonstrating His life and power in this world. His gifts in me are a part of my identity as a believer. He wants me to know the gifts I carry from Him, to grow in them, to unite with my brothers and sisters in Him, and together manifest His love, power, and goodness to this world.

Father, what gift have You given me that is to supply something needed to the rest of the Body and to this world for manifesting Your goodness and glory?

DAY 50

I AM A GOOD SOLDIER

Therefore endure hardness, as a good [admirable, choice, noble] soldier of Jesus Christ. No one engaged in warfare entangles himself with the affairs of this life, that he may please him who enlisted him as a soldier.
(2 Tim. 2:3-4 KLV)

Life is full of conflict. Earth is a battlefield. There is an enemy who continually wars against my soul. He wants to stop me in what I do. But I can't stop, I must advance. As a believer, I am part of a spiritual army of God's children on Earth. My union with Jesus has enlisted me against the destructive forces of darkness. There are lives to reach and communities to heal. There is a destiny I am to walk out. I war with a purpose.

Thankfully, I am not left alone to figure this war out. Adonai trains me for battle, to pick up my weapons of truth, to advance through adversity, to praise in the midst of difficulties, and to use His authority to cut off whatever tries to entangle me. Battles are never fun or easy, so I am told to endure nobly until victory is attained. I do not leave my position until I am assigned a new one. As I listen to my Heavenly Commander, He will show me what to do.

Father, what are You saying to me today in some hardship of life? How do You want me to fight in this battle? What is my post?

DAY 51

I AM A GREEN TREE IN GOD'S HOUSE

But as for me, I am like a green olive tree in the house of God;
I trust in the lovingkindness of God forever and ever.
(Ps. 52:8 KJV)

To be in Hashem's house is to be in His presence. In His presence is living energy that makes my life flourish in every way. There my thoughts are changed and perspectives are shifted. My very nature is transformed in His Presence as He breaks off the imprints of darkness, self-defeating patterns, and limiting mindsets so that I thrive in life and calling.

As I grow in God my life becomes useful in divine purpose. The olive tree referred to in this ancient passage took many years to mature and produce fruit but was important for producing oil. Oil was needed for energy, cooking, and for healing. In ancient Israel, olives were harvested by beating the branches so the olives would fall, be gathered, and then crushed for producing rich oil needed for enriching society.

This makes me think of the stripes laid on Yeshua's back, and how, on the cross, His very body was "pressed" for my healing. The Garden of Gethsemane where Yeshua prayed the night of His last supper was an olive Garden; Gethsemane even means "Oil-Press."

Yeshua was beaten and pressed for me, but He didn't stay pressed. He trusted the Father to bring Him though the crushing process until the oil was produced. And then Abba raised Him back to life. Father didn't fail Him.

Sometimes God takes me through pressing processes, too. It is part of maturing and being made useful as a green olive tree for Kingdom usefulness. His processes are never unto death, but unto life. I can trust His love to bring me through, and that what is produced in me will enrich others.

Abba Father, I yield all I am to You today. Your presence makes me flourish in life. Even in the pressing processes of life there is purpose and a future.

DAY 52
I AM GIVEN DIVINE AUTHORITY

Look, I have given you authority over all the power of the enemy...
(Luke 10:19 NLT)

As a believer I am given Jesus' authority over the enemy. The demonic realm is a real and present force in this world; it twists men's thoughts, cripples their bodies, and corrupts governments. It is, however, subject to the authority of Christ and Christ's authority in me as His Body. I carry Christ's name and His authority for ruling as light over the works of darkness.

I am given authority and I am to use it. I command devils to get out of my life, out of my home, and every place where He gives me authority. I can only have authority though as I am submitted to God. This includes a right submission to positions of authority He places in my life. Authorities are given to mature me for my life and calling. Submission is not an unconditional subjugation to man, but a willing cooperation to those appointed with authority to carry out the designs of God.

Father, show me how to grow in humility *and* authority today. Show me any attitude of rebellion against You or against right governing authorities. Teach me to walk in discernment regarding corrupt systems and give me Your counsel of what to do and how to pray for them.

DAY 53
I AM GIVEN THE BANNER OF TRUTH

You have given a banner to those who fear You, that it may be displayed because of the truth. Selah. (Ps. 60:4 NASB)

A banner symbolizes the government that presides over a territory and its people. The banner is a visual declaration of the presence, protection, and provision of that government over the people. It speaks of its values and type of law by which it governs.

As a believer, I am under a government of divine truth. Truth is more than words and decrees, principles and laws. It is a Person who embodies all of these and that Person is Yeshua. He *is* Truth and where He is present, He effects liberty. Many want liberty but they do not want truth, but the two cannot be separated.

When Truth is removed from a society, there goes liberty. I am given the banner of Truth to raise high as a declaration of a government that effects true liberty in my life, home, and nation.

God's people are a unified company carrying many banners of His governing presence, banners of Praise, Priesthood, Fruitfulness, and Timing, among a few. But Truth is the Captain of them all. I am not a lone ranger; I am part of a great host of redeemed ones carrying a banner of His governing Truth.

Abba Father, I revere Your Truth. Show me any place in me that is operating apart from Truth. Where do You want me to carry the government of your Truth to today? Help me to lift the banner of Truth in culture in any place where it has been trodden down in our streets as a nation. Your Truth and love is our freedom from tyranny and oppression for a life that prospers in blessing for blessing the nations.

DAY 54

I AM GOD'S PLEASURE

You are worthy, O Lord our God, to receive glory and honor and power.
For You created all things, and they exist because You created what You
pleased. (Rev. 4:11 KJV)

It pleased Hashem to make me. He called me from eternity to know Him and bring Him honor and pleasure. He envisioned my life with Him and danced with delight! The very thought of me brought pleasure to His heart before He even fashioned me in my mother's womb. He saw the beauty He would give me in place of brokenness, and the joy He would impart in place of sorrow. He saw how He would teach me to live in Him, with Him, through Him, and for Him...and all the joy and honor I would bring Him as His child. He has seen my journey of valleys and mountains, and what is yet ahead, and it brings Him pleasure because He knows my beginning and my end.

To bring someone pleasure is to bring a sense of satisfaction to them. A loving and obedient child brings a satisfaction to the heart of a parent. In the world I sought my own satisfaction and pleasure. I lived for myself. But one of the great transformations that takes place in the human heart, in my heart, through Jesus is a deep desire to satisfy the heart of God.

Father, thank You for creating me in Your love. I want to satisfy Your heart today. Jesus, teach me what satisfies Abba's heart.

DAY 55

I AM GRAFTED INTO GOD'S COVENANT
WITH ISRAEL

"Behold, days are coming," declares the Lord, "When I will make a new
covenant with the house of Israel and with the house of
Judah".... And if some of the branches were broken off,
and you, being a wild olive tree, were grafted in among
them [Israel], and with them became a partaker of the root
and fatness of the olive tree... (Jer. 31:31; Rom. 11:17 NASB)

As a believer in Yeshua, I am brought into covenant with Hashem — a covenant that He made and gave to Israel and then extended to the whole world through His Son. How marvelous is that! Because of this, my spiritual identity as a believer in Christ and child of God is intimately connected to Israel. The Church did not replace Israel, but is grafted into

God's covenant given to Israel. His faithfulness to Israel is His faithfulness to me, too.

Hashem is still working with His son. And because I am connected to Israel I pray for them, for their well-being, and for Hashem's purpose in their land. He is diligently and lovingly working with them until spiritual blindness is turned to sight and they see Yeshua and say, "Blessed is He who comes in the name of the Lord." Then Yeshua will return to Jerusalem.

Today, there is a beautiful move of God happening in the hearts of many in Israel. Hashem is not only returning His covenant people to the land He gave them, but He is returning His beloved's heart to Him through His covenant in Yeshua.

Abba Father, thank You for Your good plans for Israel! You love him and desire him with all your heart as a dear son. Today I partner with You in prayer for Your son, Israel, and the full life of the vine into which I am grafted. How do You want me to support Your good plans for them and the land You gave them, the place where Yeshua will return to rule?

DAY 56

I AM A HEALER OF LAND

For the creation waits with eager longing for the revealing of the
sons of God. For the creation was subjected to futility, not willingly,
but because of him who subjected it, in hope that the creation itself
will be set free from its bondage to corruption and obtain the freedom
of the glory of the children of God. (Rom. 8:19-21 ESV)

As a child of Hashem, I am an important part of His healing work in the Earth. Creation cries for freedom from its bondage in corruption. It is longing for God's sons and daughters to show up in freedom and glory for its restoration. Land is not a dead object but a living entity that responds to the spirit that people carry.

My work with Yeshua not only concerns the inhabitants of the land, but the land itself. It was man's sin that put the land and creation under subjection to the curse and corruption under Satan's rule. It is man's freedom that will release it. My freedom in Christ as Earth's caretaker also heals the land from its bondage!

Through the first Adam, man became the facilitators of the curse, but in Yeshua (the second Adam) redeemed mankind becomes facilitators of healing and freedom from the curse. It is a powerful responsibility to think that someone or something is waiting for me to show up with freedom and healing in my spirit because my freedom facilitates theirs. I long for God's presence and creation longs for God's presence in me. The glory I carry is more than just about my personal benefit.

Father, show me how to release freedom and healing that facilitates another's release from bondage and the curse. Show me how You want me to heal the very land I walk on.

DAY 57

I AM A HEALER OF NATIONS

Fruit trees of all kinds will grow along both sides of the river.
The leaves of these trees will never turn brown and fall, and
there will always be fruit on their branches.

There will be a new crop every month, for they are watered by
the river flowing from the Temple. The fruit will be for
food and the leaves for healing [of nations].
(Ezek. 47:12 NLT)

The Temple is the place of God's presence; His presence is like water to my spirit that makes me alive and fruitful in many ways. The fruit I bear from time with Him carries healing qualities to the world I live in. It manifests as healthy food for thought, healing words of truth and hope, and even healing power for the body. It includes ideas and strategies from His presence for impacting culture with healing where there is wounding, division, and corruption.

Father calls me to drink daily from the water of His Word and presence so it will produce fruit in me in every season of life, fruit that gives life to others. Different seasons produce different things, whether as a deeper joy, enlarged vision, increased wisdom, or broader outreach. The fruit of God's Spirit in me produces what is pleasing to Him, and a needed richness for healing the world around me.

Abba, what is the fruit You want to see developed in my life today? How do You want to use it to heal my home, community, and nation?

DAY 58

I AM AN HEIR OF GOD

Now you are no longer a slave but God's own child. And since you are
His child, God has made you His heir. (Gal. 4:7 NLT)

I serve my Father, but I am not His slave; I am His child and heir. An heir is one who receives the wealth of a parent and with it inherent responsibilities. Jesus is the appointed heir of all things from the Father and in Him I receive an inheritance, too. I have received a spiritual wealth for living and prospering in divine purpose on Earth and for eternity. A spiritual wealth translates into blessings in every dimension both spiritual and natural.

The riches of salvation are mine. Deliverance and eternal life are mine. Healing is mine. Revelation is mine. Authority is mine. Wisdom is mine. Blessings are mine. And with them comes the responsibilities for governing in life and in all that He has for me to do with the riches He has given me.

Abba, thank You for bestowing on me such riches! How do You want me to use them wisely today?

DAY 59

I AM AN HONORABLE VESSEL

And the vessel that He made of clay was marred in the hand of the
Potter; so he made it again into another vessel, as it seemed good to the
Potter to make. (Jer. 18:4 NKJV)

Hashem takes the brokenness of my life and remakes me into something new, something good, something beautiful and honorable. The old life marred by sin was not useful for Him. But in Christ, I am a new vessel fit for His use. The word "made" means to fashion with deliberation for ordaining to an appointed function. God's fashioning in my life is for ordaining me to an appointed use. There is a specific service that He, in His wisdom and love, has appointed me to accomplish, something that will bring honor to His name.

Some people look at another's ministry or work and want to be them. They don't see the value they carry in who God fashioned them to be to bring Him honor in a way only they can bring. It is a lie of the enemy that works to make them disown their worth and thus neglect the honor that comes from that unique worth. I cannot bring God honor trying to be someone else. God wants me to authentically be who I am and celebrate how He has fashioned me! This brings Him honor.

Abba, teach me to bring You honor as a vessel pliable in Your hands and carefully shaped for Your plans of service for me.

DAY 60

I AM HEALED

For I am the Lord who heals you. (Ex. 15:26 NKJV)

God heals my spirit and soul, and He also heals my body. He Himself declared it to be so — He is my healer, and He is not a liar. Jesus' work on the cross made healing available to me in every way. When He was on Earth He healed people, and He still heals today. He is still present to heal through His presence, angelic ministry, and through His Body that is gifted and anointed to heal! Miracles have not ceased. Healing has not ceased.

Psalm 103 admonishes me to not forget the benefits and works of God's presence with me including, His forgiveness, healing from all diseases, deliverance, and renewal. These are part of His covenant with me. He wants me to walk in them and experience them as His child. He is the eternal healing fountain that has not ceased to flow. He invites me to come and drink of Him for my spirit, soul, and body.

Father, thank You for Your healing grace. Your Word commands me to not forget this blessing that You have declared for me.

DAY 61

I AM HIGHLY ESTEEMED

The Lord has appeared of old to me, saying: "Yes, I have loved
you with an everlasting love; therefore with lovingkindness
I have drawn you." (Jer. 31:3 NKJV)

To esteem someone is to regard them with worth and value. It is to cherish their life and relationship as a treasure. God highly esteems my relationship with Him as a treasure. It is this understanding that empowers me to come to Him always with confidence.

God esteems me and delights in me. He is not angry with me or indifferent towards me. He knows my weaknesses and yet He is not put off with me. He delights in my nearness to Him. He delights watching my development as His child. My humble obedience delights Him. He acts favorably towards me, even when He is disciplining and correcting me because He esteems me as His delightful child.

People and circumstances can sometimes make me feel unvalued and worthless. They can make me feel like anything but a treasure. When I believe that kind of report about myself, my heart shuts down, I close in,

I navel-gaze, and I self-comfort in wrong ways. I was created to be loved and valued and express the same to others.

I was created to be celebrated and delighted in, and to celebrate those around me like He does. God wants His treasuring view of me to trump over every earthly and demonic opinion about me so that I live confidently and unwavering from His perspective and not another's. He also wants me to see others from that same perspective in how He treasures them, and to treat them accordingly.

Father, thank You for esteeming me so highly in Your love and for delighting in me. Show me any place where I am living by a low opinion of myself that is not Your opinion that I might break agreement with it and accept Your regard of me. Show me where I need to esteem others with Your opinion of them, too.

DAY 62

I AM AN INTERCESSOR

Even those I will bring to My holy mountain and make them joyful in My house of prayer. Their burnt offerings and their sacrifices will be acceptable on My altar; for My house will be called a house of prayer for all the peoples. (Isa. 56:7 NASB)

The word intercessor means someone who meets with another for the purpose of seeking their favor regarding a critical issue. It also means to strike against, to reach the mark. God's house is a place of intercession, entreaty, and supplication on behalf of others. God wants me to meet with Him about the concerns of others for the purpose of uniting Heaven with Earth.

As the body of the Great Intercessor, Jesus, I am to meet with God about the issues happening on Earth. I am not to be indifferent or unbelieving. I am to step into an encounter with His presence to bring Heaven's strike against injustice and unrighteousness that corrupts lives and holds them captive. I am to meet with Him for the purpose of effecting His will and justice in the Earth as Earth's caretaker. Intercession is a place of worship and prayer before the righteous Judge of All, getting His decrees, and also the actions I am to take accordingly to hit the mark.

Jesus, teach me to meet with You in the place of intercession. Earth is waiting for Heaven's strike.

DAY 63

I AM JOYFUL

*I will be filled with joy because of You. I will sing praises to
Your name, O Most High. (Ps. 9:2 NLT)*

Nothing pleases a parent more than a happy child. As Abba's child, my joy delights Him. Joy releases an internal strength of spirit, an optimistic outlook, and a deep sense of well-being. Joy empowers hope and vision, and it glorifies God as an expression of trust in His care.

Worries and fears can drain my sense of well-being and deplete my emotional strength, clouding my thoughts with confusion. I can't see, can't hear, can't think, and can't move! In the Old Testament, King David understood the power of joy and so encouraged Himself continually in the Lord. David faced many intense battles and personal challenges and learned that to overcome in life, he had to look to God for His joy rather than to circumstances. He also learned that the best way to take off the cloak of heaviness was to release joy by singing praise.

The song of praise (not just saying it) releases a resonating power within my spirit that lifts my soul to see God as being bigger than the problem. Because He is. Hope returns. Vision clears, and with it a sense of well-being and strength knowing that God is with me. As I sing praise, God shows up!

Father, thank You for joy. Teach me today to break free of any spirit of sorrow and walk in Your strength through singing praise.

DAY 64

I AM JUSTIFIED

*And such were some of you. But you were washed, but you were
sanctified, but you were justified in the name of the Lord Jesus and by
the Spirit of our God. (I Cor. 6:11 NKJV)*

To be justified means to be viewed and pronounced as being righteous before God on the conditions laid down by Him. In the case of humanity, the condition of justification can never be fulfilled through mere human endeavor, but only through faith in the blood of Jesus. His sacrifice provided the legal acquittal from guilt for all mankind.

Justification is an acquittal from guilt that is experienced and effectual to all who put their trust in Jesus.

Justification is the position of not being condemned. Romans 8:1-5 says there is no longer any condemnation to those who are in Christ, those who no longer live with a mind set on the flesh but who conduct their life according to the Spirit.

Satan uses condemnation and accusation to keep me bound in my mind, ever looking at my weaknesses, never measuring up. But as a believer, I stand justified — just as if I had not sinned. I am free from condemnation and guilt so that I can now grow in grace into all that I am called to be. My righteousness is not in my ability to perform or be perfect, but in Him who is working out His own image in me.

Jesus, thank You for justification. Show me any place where I am trying to perform my own way into right standing, today.

DAY 65

I AM A KINGDOM AMBASSADOR

So we are Christ's ambassadors; God is making His appeal through us.
We speak for Christ when we plead, "Come back to God!"
(2 Cor. 5:20 NLT)

An ambassador is an official diplomat who represents their home country while working and living in the country to which they have been appointed. An ambassador is a leader who listens and observes what is going on in the host country while serving the interests of their home government. An ambassador deals in legal issues.

I am God's ambassador here on Earth. I have a heavenly assignment to represent Adonai's Kingdom and His legal interests in my family, community, and nation. After all, He made them and everything belongs to Him. I make His comfort, admonition, and power known to the nations as His governing representative. The nations belong to Him and I am appointed to protect and develop the nation He assigns me to.

Abba, teach me to represent Your interests in my home, community, region and my nation.

DAY 66

I AM A KINGDOM PRIEST

And has made us kings and priests to His God and Father, to Him be glory and dominion forever and ever. Amen (Rev. 1:6 NKJV)

Kings and priests are positions of authority — one deals with issues regarding the Earth and the other in matters of Heaven. God designed these two mantels to operate together, for Heaven and Earth were always meant to operate together, as one. It is why Jesus — King of Kings, High Priest, and Ruler of the Nations — prayed, "Father, Your will be done on Earth as it is in Heaven."

Centuries ago when God gave the promised land to Israel, Mt. Zion was made the center where He established the unity of these two powers. Mt. Zion was the place of the Lord's holy temple *and* King David's palace. On the top of the mount, the glory of God dwelled in the priestly house of worship, and just a few feet away and not quite as high on the mount was David's palace of kingly authority…Heaven's presence and Earth's rule.

David understood the important unity of both and that his authority was only strong as it came from intimacy with God. He was not a priest by natural calling, but he was a spiritual priest who ministered to God in worship, and thus He made worship and the presence of God the most important thing in his life and calling as a ruler. Worship came first.

The restoration of Earth requires the restoration of Earth's alignment with Heaven; it requires the presence of God's glory. As a believer, I am both a spiritual king and a priest. My authority in Christ flows from the altar of worship where I stand as a priest ministering to Him.

As a priest, I stand in His presence and minister to Him through worship, prayer, and intercession. I bring the issues of men's hearts before His throne for the purpose of reconciling a broken Earth with Heaven's healing. I meet with God in partnership regarding what is broken down and separate from Him. As I worship, He also mantles me with authority regarding my call and labor for territory.

Part of my worship and ruling is through identification repentance that cleanses the land and reunites regions and people groups in forgiveness, restoring them to the presence of God.

Father, teach me today to worship and rule — to minister to You and to unite Earth with Heaven.

DAY 67

I AM A KINGDOM WARRIOR

You are as…awesome as an army with banners.
(Song of Songs 6:4 NASB)

As a believer, I am both gentle and kind…and fierce! As a Kingdom ambassador I gather information and work with legal issues in the courts of Heaven. As a Kingdom warrior, I move on the decrees of God with His authority and presence and ride with Heaven's power for releasing justice.

Like all military companies, warriors in Adonai's army have a specific assignment, position and rank. They operate within a regiment and operate with a specific purpose in an appointed locale. I have an assignment, position, and rank from God for Kingdom purposes. My gifts, calling, and alignments are given me for my assigned position and warfare.

We like beds of roses, but the truth is we are in a spiritual battle for planet Earth. We have a very real enemy who uses people to effect his evil schemes. My place as a warrior is to be watchful and active, even to the laying down of my life.

Father, teach me to both operate in the courts of Heaven and to also war with the decrees of Adonai as I carry Your government into my region. What is my assignment? What is my position? And what are the relationship alignments You have for me in this season? Teach me to have a willing heart to lay down my life.

DAY 68
I AM A LIGHT IN THIS WORLD

For you were once darkness, but now you are light in the Lord.
Live as children of light. (Eph. 5:8 NIV)

Light is needed for dispelling darkness and empowering clear vision. Light also has many healing properties. It empowers growth and inspires an emotional sense of well-being. My life before Christ was one of darkness — sick, without vision, separate from God. But now I am light and I have a Heavenly charge to walk as light to bring healing to others, empower their growth, and lift them with a sense of well-being in Christ.

I am not here to waste my years in self-seeking pleasures, but to walk in the light and radiate the light of God's glory. Darkness is not my identity; the Light is.

Jesus wants to energize others through my words and actions. People everywhere are crying out for light, hope, and a way out of their darkness.

Jesus, who do You want to enlighten through me today?

DAY 69

I AM A LOVER OF GOD

*Love the Lord your God with all your heart and with all your
soul and with all your mind and with all your strength.*
(Mark 12:30 NIV)

I am the desire of Hashem's affections and He is the desire of mine. Love seeks connection! Love is not satisfied to simply watch at a distance but it longs for active engagement. Hashem loves me wholeheartedly and seeks for me to love Him in return.

Hashem is a consuming fire who seeks fiery love — a love for Him that is with all my heart, soul, mind, and strength. He knows my human love stumbles with good intentions but often lacks follow through; and so the Holy Spirit pours divine love into me so that I can love God more fully with a love that transforms my affections, thoughts, goals, and dreams. And so I live my life as a lover of God, rather than a lover of self or of this world.

Lord, I want to connect wholeheartedly with You in love! How can I love You more fully today with my thoughts, actions, desires, and even my emotions? Where am I not loving You fully?

DAY 70

I AM A LOVER OF PEOPLE

Love your neighbor as yourself. (Mark 12:31 NIV)

God says I am to love Him, and others as myself. Loving God means loving people, too. In Him, I am not to separate the two. I am not to shut my eyes to their needs and concerns. I am not to harbor bitterness or bias, but to love them with His love. The Apostle John wrote that if I do not love others, I do not know God; my love for Him must manifest as love for others, too.

Saint Paul described love as being kind, patient, and not jealous. It doesn't brag, is not arrogant, is not rude, is not self-seeking, and it is not easily provoked, and does not hold a grudge. It is easy to love God who is perfect and whom I cannot see versus people who are visibly imperfect...including myself! But if I am to walk with God and know His love, I must let His love flow to me and through me to others. This means I must love myself as well.

Father, who do I need to love in a greater way today? How do You want me to express it? Do I need to love and care for my spirit, soul, and body in a healthier way, too? What would that look like?

DAY 71

I AM A LOVER OF TRUTH

And with all wicked deception for those who are perishing, because they refused to love the truth and so be saved.
(2 Thess. 2:10 ESV)

To be a lover of God is to love the Truth, for He is the God is Truth. Yeshua is Truth and the Holy Spirit is the Spirit of Truth. Truth is light that contains within its nature the power to heal, restore, and set free. Divine truth is the source of salvation from destruction for an individual, as well as for a family or nation. God says that the heart that will not believe the truth is evil and full of darkness that leads to ruin. When the love of truth is replaced by a love for deception, freedom is lost while corruption and wickedness ensue, and thus ruin.

Father, fill my heart with a love for the truth today. Show me any place where I am trusting in lies and compromising with deceit. Show me how to sow the love of truth into my sphere of influence.

DAY 72

I AM LIFTED UP

The Lord opens the eyes of the blind; the Lord raises up those who are bowed down. (Ps. 146:8b NASB)

To be bowed down is to be overcome with the weight of cares and the burden of a circumstance too heavy for me to bear. It is to be overwhelmed so that hopelessness is all I see. Hopelessness is the dread felt in seeing no way out of some trouble. But God is the God of hope. And just as He opened the eyes of Elisha's servant to see a heavenly host around them to give them victory, so God lifts my eyes to see that He is with me, and that with Him there is a way out, a way up, and a way forward. "This season too shall pass," He says, "and meanwhile, I am at work."

God lifts my vision to see that He is greater than my difficulty and that He has a vast supply to help me with by myriad means. He is not limited in any way to bring me help. He will send His presence. He will send angels. He will not leave my soul in Sheol. Lack of clarity and vision and being bowed down is not what He desires for me as His child. He has something better for me, and so He restores vision and lifts my face to Hope.

Father, thank You that You will not leave me in a dark night forever. You do not want me to live despairingly and overwhelmed with problems, for it is easy to do. And so You lift my face to look upward to You with hope, for as surely as winter turns to spring, morning will come and with it the refreshing rain, and the light of a new day.

DAY 73
I AM A MESSENGER OF SALVATION

> How beautiful on the mountains are the feet of the messenger who brings good news, the good news of peace and salvation, the news that the God of Israel reigns! (Isa. 52:7 NLT)

A messenger is one who goes places and brings news. He is like the pony express sent to deliver a message to someone. As a believer, I am an apostolic messenger of God's peace and salvation to others. Peace (Heb. "Shalom") means wholeness, completeness, nothing lacking, nothing missing. It also means the authority that destroys chaos.

God wants me to take His message to those in chaos, turmoil, and darkness…to those who are missing something and are groaning, wondering where God is. He wants them to know that He hears their prayers, He sees, and that He is present to help them. He is on the throne and His scepter is extended toward them in favor. Adonai sends me to proclaim His favor to them *and* His vengeance on His enemies. It a message for me, too!

The year of God's favor towards man and vengeance on His enemy came into the world through Jesus Christ. One day that vengeance on Satan and the host that serves his evil works will culminate in righteous judgment and full justice. Meanwhile, I am God's messenger of peace and salvation. He is on the throne and He is present for restoring what is lacking and destroying chaos!

Father, who do You want me to be bring Your message to today?

DAY 74
I AM A MINISTER OF GOD

You will be spoken of as ministers of our God. (Isa. 61:6 NASB)

A minister is one who serves, one who supplies something that is needed. I am a minister of the gospel, a servant of the Most High. I serve others by being a supply of God's goodness to them, a supply that comes from His presence. Yeshua came to serve, not to be served. This does not mean that I do not receive from others as that is important, too! It does mean that I am not here to live a self-pleasing life, but to minister life to the world around me.

Ministry is not about "doing" but about "being." It is an overflow of the divine life in me pouring out through me. His Kingdom has come with life and power to bring a divine supply to people, families, businesses, and governments. Sometimes bringing heavenly supply is not convenient for my schedule or comfortable for my otherwise personal desires. But being a minister means being willing to see a need and bring a heavenly supply to it as Holy Spirit leads me. It might be prayer, encouragement, or food, or something else.

Abba, who do You want me to serve today and bring a supply of Your goodness? The store clerk? My boss? My neighbor?

DAY 75
I AM A MOUNTAIN CLIMBER

Ah, I hear my lover coming! He is leaping over the mountains, bounding over the hills…My lover said to me, "Rise up, my darling! Come away with me, my fair one!" (Songs 2:8, 10 NLT)

A mountain can refer to a place of open vision, a governing structure, or an insurmountable obstacle. Jesus moves effortlessly on them all! Here He is bounding over high places calling His darling, me, to rise from the lowlands and come up higher to a place of fresh vision with Him. His ease tells me that what has been a difficulty and obstacle for me until now will no longer hold me down or hold me back. It is time to come up higher and rule the mountain rather than let it stand in my way.

Ps. 18:33 says that He makes me surefooted like a deer, enabling me to stand on mountain heights. Climbing mountains takes incredible effort and strength. It is not a task for the frail or fearful. But Jesus says that He empowers my ability to move in ways that I could not before or on my own. He is calling me to come with Him to new heights and see from new perspectives the horizon of a new day.

I have been through the valley of the shadow of death. I have dwelled in the valley of decision long enough. I am not to live there. It is time to come up higher. He who lovingly calls me will enable me to rise and move with Kingdom movement. The old is gone, the new has come.

Thank You, Yeshua, that You beckon me to come higher with You. You enable me to climb places of impossibility and see new things with new perspective. What mountain do You want me to climb and leap on with You today?

DAY 76

I AM MARKED WITH DIVINE PROMISE

In Him you also trusted, after you heard the word of truth, the gospel of your salvation; in whom also, having believed, you were sealed with the Holy Spirit of promise. (Eph. 1:13 NKJV)

To seal something is to mark it as belonging to you. Kings have royal seals that authenticate a possession or decree as being theirs. As a believer, I am marked with the Holy Spirit as one belonging to Hashem. I am a divine possession! I am authenticated in the heavenly realm as being reserved for divine purpose and keeping. The divine seal of decree stamped on my life removes all doubt about whose I am before Him. I am reserved for Him forever. I am marked for Him.

Hashem knows those who are His. No one can take away my position in Him. No created thing can remove the mark and presence of the Holy Spirit from me…no death, persecution, trouble, or accusation.

Father, thank You for making me Yours and sealing me with Your Spirit forever.

DAY 77

I AM A NEW CREATION

*Therefore, if anyone is in Christ, he is a new creation; old things have passed away, and look, new things have come.
(2 Cor. 5:17 HCSB)*

As a believer I am a new creation. I am not the same as I was before I believed in Christ. I do not live the same, think the same, I do not even look the same. My relationships are different. My attire may be different. Certainly my activities and attitude are different. I have a new heart and a new spirit. I have new thoughts and desires, new aspirations and new vision. I have new purpose. The old life is dead and buried with Christ.

I have risen with Christ into a new life of living for the Father and all that I am as His child. I have a new dream with new connections, and a joy of His presence with me. I have left the life of being an earthbound worm, living in the dirt, to rise with Christ and soar with Him in the atmosphere of Heaven. I am no longer trodden down or trodden on; I have the wings of an eagle. I am a new creation!

Jesus, thank You for this new life! Teach me today to use my wings to soar in prayer and in Your presence. Who do You want me to share this glorious new creation experience with today?

DAY 78

I AM NOT AFRAID

For God has not given us a spirit of fear, but of power, and of love, and of a sound mind. (2 Tim. 1:7 NKJV)

God is love; He works through love. Satan works through fear…the fear of the past, regrets, tomorrow's uncertainties, current troubles, and the fear of people. Satan exploits my concerns about finances, health, and family, and anything else he can use to bind me with anxiety, worry, and fear. Fear isn't just a feeling, it is a spirit. It comes to torment with unsound thinking.

God says that He has not given me a spirit of fear but of power, love, and a sound mind. God gives me His power and love to remove the presence of timidity and fear. Love removes fearful thoughts about my past, present, and future. Immersing myself in God's ever present love breaks my fear of abandonment, failure, and people's opinions. I have inner power from God to take hold of my thoughts, to command fear to go, and to roll on to Him all that concerns me for He is in charge of my care (1 Pet. 5:7). In Hashem's love I am not timid or fearful; I am fearless!

Abba, thank You for Your love and power. What fear do I need to command to leave me today?

DAY 79

I AM NOT FORSAKEN

You shall no longer be termed Forsaken, nor shall your land any more be termed Desolate; but you shall be called Hephzibah ["My delight is in her"], and your land Beulah["Married"]; for the Lord delights in you, and your land shall be married. (Isa. 62:4 NKJV)

The human heart looks for faithful friendships and a loyal lover who is true. We were made in God's image for such relationships. But in a broken world, betrayal and abandonment are experiences all too common place and these can wound the heart deeply. Many lives are devastated by the pain of abandonment and the destruction it leaves. Sometimes it makes us see God that way, too. But God is a Faithful and True lover.

God addresses my fear of abandonment by promising that He will never walk away from me, leave me behind, or abandon me. He will not forget me or desert me. His love is loyal because I am His delight. He is committed to me, no matter what. His delight in me keeps me always before His eyes. He has plans for my life and His intentions towards me are good. And so, I am not abandoned; I am kept because I am dearly loved.

Father, thank You that You do not throw me away. You will never do that to me. Let every place of abandonment be filled now with the reality that though forsaken by a person, for whatever reason, I am not forsaken by You. Your love is faithful.

DAY 80

I AM NOT IGNORANT

Now whom you forgive I forgive also…lest Satan should take advantage of us; for we are not ignorant of his devices. (2 Cor. 2:11)

Satan has evil purposes and two of his most used weapons are offense and unforgiveness. I am not to be ignorant of this matter. His goal is to shut me down and lock me up in a the torment of bitterness, resentment, and anger because of what someone did…whether directly to me or to someone I love. Depression, too, can be rooted in suppressed anger over something I could not control. Unforgiveness is a dark prison.

God forgives and says that I must forgive, too. It is part of being a believer in Jesus who said, "Father, forgive them for they know not what they do." Jesus knew that His own adversaries and hateful offenders were people operating with darkened minds, even though they were religious leaders! But He committed everything to His Father who worked gloriously through it all.

When I forgive, I release the hand of God to work in the hearts of all involved and bring about His justice and redemption. Unforgiveness is a dark cell that incarcerates *me* (not them); it gives my mind over to tormenting thoughts. But forgiveness is the open door that releases me, and thus my ability to hear from God to get His heart on the matter, and then take Spirit-led actions accordingly. Forgiveness is not injustice, but it does free me from an internal torment of dark thoughts that seeks personal justice my way. Forgiveness releases peace in me for moving forward.

Father, I let go of any unforgiveness today. I commit every situation to You for Your justice to be worked out, and redemption released. As You have forgiven me, so I forgive others, not letting the enemy have a foothold in my heart and life through offense. Help me to not be ignorant of any place where the enemy is trying to pull me into an offense or holding on to a grudge.

DAY 81

I AM NOT OF THIS WORLD

And do not be conformed to this world, but be transformed by the renewing of your mind, that you may prove what is that good and acceptable and perfect will of God. (Rom. 12:2 NKJV)

Yeshua said that His Kingdom was not of this world. He Himself was in the world but was not of the world. He didn't think like the world. He thought like His Father. The world could not even discern who He was or the Light He carried.

The world is under a dominion of darkness. It is a world of lusts and pride. It is an evil current that wants to take me with it. God says that I carry another dominion and I am not to conform my life to the world's ways that bow to the voice of Satan's influence and directives. I am to live God's way and *be* His influence to this world.

I am to love people but not conform my values and goals to the way they may operate. My values and character are to be one with Christ. I must renew my mind continually to the truth of God's Word and presence in everything so that I can live out my life doing the will of my Father in Heaven. I am to influence others with the current of Heaven.

Abba, is there anywhere in my life that I am operating by the ways of this world and its lusts? Help me to see and be honest so that any heart corrections can be made today.

DAY 82

I AM NURTURED BY GOD'S LOVE

He has brought me to His banquet hall, and His banner over me is love. (Song of Solomon 2:4 KJV)

There is a saying that we are what we eat. Nutrients, or the lack of them, impact our whole being—physical, intellectual, and even spiritual. As a believer, God has a rich table called His Spirit and His Word from which He wants to nourish me every day under the care of His love. Eating the garbage of worldly passions, ambitions, resentments and compromises, corrupts the intricate systems of who I am as a believer. Eating from the junk of ungodly programs, music, and philosophies tears down the fabric of my spirit, soul, and even body.

Hashem, however, has high frequency food for nurturing my spirit and soul with truth and love that also brings health to my physical being! Just as good food is necessary for physical growth, so is God's Word and love necessary for my full potential and development in every way.

Abba, thank You for the table of good things You have for me. What unloving foods of thought have I been eating that need to be removed from my mental and spiritual diet today?

DAY 83
I AM A NURTURER OF MY FAITH

Now for this very reason also, applying all diligence, in your faith supply moral excellence, and in your moral excellence [purity], knowledge, and in your knowledge, self-control, and in your self-control, perseverance, and in your perseverance, godliness, and in your godliness, brotherly kindness, and in your kindness, love.

For if these qualities are yours and are increasing, they will keep you from being useless or unfruitful in the knowledge of our Lord Jesus Christ. For he who lacks these qualities is blind or short-sighted, having forgotten his purification from his former sins. (2 Peter 1:5-8 NASB)

Faith is a gift from God, a seed to be nurtured and developed. The Apostle Peter taught seven critical elements needed for developing my life in faith. They are: moral purity, knowledge, self-control, perseverance, respect towards God, brotherly kindness, and love. These specific qualities carry empowering nutrients for my spiritual growth and a fruitful life with vision.

The opposite is also true, Peter says; moral impurity, ignorance of God, impatience, lack of self-control, irreverence of the Holy, or lack in compassion and love, make me dull in spiritual matters, blind to the purposes of God, and unfruitful.

My personal character and faith requires my diligent attention. No one can grow in character and faith for me. I must take the Word of God and read it, asking Holy Spirit who lives in me to teach me from it. I must open its pages and ask Him to speak to me from what I read, and to change me where needed. Under Holy Spirit's tutelage I learn what it is to be morally pure, to know God intimately, and to be in control of myself instead of being jerked around by my own selfish passions. I learn to be kind, to persevere, and to love.

Abba, I desire faith that has vision and fruitfulness in my life. Show me where my faith is lacking any quality needed for my full development as Your child.

DAY 84
I AM AN OBJECT OF HIS COMPASSION

He also made them objects of compassion in the presence of
all their captors. (Ps. 106:46)

Hashem has set His love on me. His eyes are focused, seeing my life as the object of His compassion. I am not overlooked. Whatever is going on in my life, whatever is surrounding me trying to entrap or destroy me, He sees, He cares, and He moves to do something about it! He doesn't leave me to the destructive schemes of the enemy. His eyes are ever on me.

Scripture says that Hashem looks throughout the Earth that He may strongly support those whose heart is completely His (2 Chron. 16:9). I see my weakness, but He sees my heart and the battle against me. When I cry out to Him, He comes to work on my behalf, because He has set His kindness on me.

Father, thank You for the display of Your compassion over me when the enemy surrounds me. Where do I need to trust You more? Who do You want me to encourage regarding Your compassion for them today?

DAY 85
I AM ONE WITH CHRIST

Who can know the Lord's thoughts? Who knows enough to teach
Him? But we understand these things, for we have the mind of Christ.
(1 Cor. 2:16 NLT)

To be one with someone is to have the same heart, mind, and spirit. To be one with God is to know His heart and thoughts and be in agreement with Him. It is to live in His presence. As Yeshua's body, the Holy Spirit makes His thoughts and desires known to me so that I can move through circumstances with His mind rather than leaning on my own. Sometimes I think I know what's best, but then He says, "Really? You know better than Me?" And then I remember God's conversations with Job.

God does not need me to tell Him what to do or how things should be done. Rather, He teaches me and shows me how things really are, and gives me the wisdom for the moment I am in. Seeking His presence and leaning on His mind rather than my own makes me move as one with Him, and not as a disjointed member of His body.

Yeshua, thank You that You know best. Show me where I need to surrender my thoughts to You today to be one with You.

DAY 86
I AM A PARTAKER OF GLOBAL RICHES

You will eat the wealth of nations, and in their riches you will boast. (Isa. 61:6 NASB)

To eat the wealth of nations is to partake of their strength. This can refer to finances, military strength, provision, and any other means through which my life is enriched through the cultures and goods within nations. Being enriched by the nations is a promise of God to His people, including me.

This is not about selfish gain through ungodly means or forceful taking by an unjust means or war. This promise is a spiritual reward of sowing and reaping. I sow to the Spirit and I reap blessings above and in the Earth.

Every nation has an expression of God laced within it — an expression that is rich in blessings, strengths, insights, creativity, and hidden wealth in the land waiting to be rightly released to glorify God and enrich the people of Earth. Poverty and lack are not from God, and as I honor covenant with Him and sow His love and care into the nations, I will also reap the richness of their strengths.

Yeshua, how do You want me to sow Your blessings into the nations today? As I do, may there be a return of reward in wealth the way You desire for me.

DAY 87

I AM A PEACEMAKER

Blessed are the peacemakers, for they shall be called sons of God. (Matt. 5:9 NKJV)

A peacemaker is one who goes into a situation to bring unity and peace. A peacemaker brings wisdom and counsel to remove chaos and establish well-being between two parties. The term peace (Heb. "Shalom") means authority over chaos.

I have experienced the presence of Christ in my life as the Peacemaker who removed chaos in my soul and brought unity between my Creator and me. The Prince of Peace has restored order in my inner man, alignment with Heaven, and well-being in my relationships so that my life prospers. In turn, I am to be a peacemaker, too, bringing God's wisdom, counsel, and presence into situations where confusion, turmoil and disorder are wreaking havoc in lives and culture. I am called to minister His Shalom in this world through my words, actions, and presence.

Jesus, show me today where You want to bring Your counsel and wisdom through me…as a peace that removes chaos and facilitates unity so those who are at odds can reconcile and prosper as You desire.

DAY 88

I AM A POSSESSOR OF LAND

See, I have placed the land before you; go in and possess the land which the Lord swore to give to your fathers, to Abraham, to Isaac, and to Jacob, to them and their descendants after them. (Deut. 1:8 NASB)

To possess the land means to move in, remove current governing structures, and establish a new governing structure for a new cultural expression. It requires an "ownership" mentality, whether through literal purchase or business, but certainly through presence and influence. Possessing land is a Heavenly charge to Adonai's people for establishing His Kingdom on Earth as it is in Heaven. Again, it is the same commandment from the beginning that Elohim gave to Adam to keep and cultivate the land. For Adam in the Garden of Eden, there was nothing to remove (except the crafty serpent), but for ancient Israel it meant removing the presence of ungodly covenants and worship. In their place, Israel was to establish the altar of the Lord and covenant with Him as the land's governing influence.

Establishing a kingdom involves the establishment of worship and covenant. This applies to both the Kingdom of God and the kingdom of Satan. Ancient Israel spent many years in a land of ungodly covenants and idol worship (Egypt) followed by 40 years of wandering in a wilderness. For them to enter the new day of possessing land, they had to shift in their thinking out of a bondage mindset (unbelief), as well as out of a "passing through" mentality in the wilderness. They had to put on an "ownership of promise" mindset, and with it a will to fight for prophetic promise and destiny…both theirs and the land's that God had appointed to them.

People and land both have a prophetic promise and destiny from God. I must move from unbelief and a "passing through" mindset to an "ownership" perspective regarding prophetic promise and destiny — both for me and where Adonai places me. Only then will I have vision to fight for it through intercession and Spirit-led labor for seeing demonic structures removed and God's life-giving Kingdom established in my region and nation. This battle to possess land involves repentance, cleansing the land, worship and prayer, and ministering the love and power of God to people. As a believer, I join Jesus' ownership of Earth as a present part of possessing land.

Father, how do You want me to fight and possess prophetic promises today for me, my family, the land and nation? What are those prophetic promises?

DAY 89
I AM PART OF AN ETERNAL KINGDOM

Your Kingdom is an everlasting Kingdom, and Your dominion endures throughout all generations. (Ps. 145:13 NKJV)

It is glorious to think how God links my human life to His vast eternal plans! The bigness of it is beyond comprehension. His Kingdom is forever; every thought and action that I take now on Earth and that is aligned with His Kingdom will remain forever. As a believer, I am building with Him something that will endure time.

The things of this world will surely pass away, but what is sown to the Spirit abides forever. I am not simply alive for a few years on Earth, I am part of a Kingdom that will never end.

Father, thank You for making me a part of Your Kingdom! Teach me to sow my life into what lasts forever, and in so doing reap an eternal reward.

DAY 90

I AM PART OF GOD'S FAMILY

*For this reason I bow my knees to the Father of our
Lord Jesus Christ, from whom the whole family in heaven and
earth is named. (Eph. 3:14-15 NKJV)*

God is a family: Father, Son, and Comforter, and with a host of children born of His Spirit. Family is about intimate connection and presence. God created me for connection, and family is the most important connection of all. Loneliness is a debilitating feeling of abandonment and aloneness that mankind was never created to experience. It is to be without the presence of another. In the Garden, Elohim said it was not good for man to be alone. We need family. We need Elohim as a Holy Parent and we need one another. And so He brings me into a family.

Psalm 68:6 says that God makes a home for the lonely and connects them with family—intimate relationships that share life, love, and caring for one another. When we come into this world we are born into a family. For those who have no family, God gives them a family. He brings people into our lives to be family to us, such as spiritual parents and friends who are like a dear brother or sister with whom we share a kindred-heart, purpose, and companionship. God created our need for connection and so He gives us Himself and others.

Father, thank You for family. Teach me to be a loving family member to both my earthly and spiritual relationships. Both need my love and care. Who do I need to connect with better today?

DAY 91

I AM PROSPEROUS

*And all these blessings shall come upon you and overtake you,
because you obey the voice of the Lord your God: You will be blessed
in the city and blessed in the country. Your children and your crops will
be blessed. The offspring of your herds and flocks will be blessed.
Wherever you go and whatever you do, you will be blessed. The Lord
will conquer your enemies when they attack you. They will attack you
from one direction, but they will scatter from you in seven!*

The Lord will guarantee a blessing on everything you do and will fill your storehouses with grain. The Lord your God will bless you in the land He is giving you if you obey the commands of the Lord your God and walk in His ways, the Lord will establish you as His holy people as He swore He would do.

Then all the nations of the world will see that you are a people claimed by the LORD, and they will stand in awe of you. The LORD will give you prosperity in the land He swore to your ancestors to give you, blessing you with many children, numerous livestock, and abundant crops.

The LORD will send rain at the proper time from his rich treasury in the heavens and will bless all the work you do. You will lend to many nations, but you will never need to borrow from them.

If you listen to these commands of the LORD your God that I am giving you today, and if you carefully obey them, the LORD will make you the head and not the tail, and you will always be on top and never at the bottom. (Deut. 28:2-13)

What amazing promises I am given as a believer…blessings, He says, that will overtake my life as I walk in loving obedience to Him. To prosper means to advance, succeed, and make progress, as opposed to stagnation and withering. I am not a stagnant or withering believer. Hashem wants me to be prosperous and not in lack, to be fruitful and advancing in life rather than living as a victim. He wants me to use my prosperity for blessing others. The promise of blessing as I walk with Him is for a purpose. A Kingdom purpose. Never a selfish purpose.

Father, thank You for Your deep desire towards me to make me prosperous, so that I, in turn, can bless others. Who do You want me to bless today with the prosperity You've given me?

DAY 92

I AM A RADIANT ONE

They looked to Him and were radiant, and their faces were not ashamed. (Ps. 34:5 NKJV)

What I focus on and give my attention to creates a resonating emotion, thought, attitude and perspective that impacts everything in my life. If I focus on negative things, I become negative. If I focus on something I'm afraid of, I become fearful. But when I focus my thoughts on God, experience His presence, and trust His love and care, I am filled with a hope that gives wings to my soul. It is a focus that energizes me with light!

Fixing my eyes on The Lord who loves me, drives the shadows away from my mind. Looking to Him who is my faithful help inspires my thoughts with endless possibilities of just how He will come to my rescue and lead me into breakthrough. His greatness towards me makes me confident in Him; I will not be put to shame for trusting Him.

In Song of Solomon 6:10, there is a symbolic description of the bride as being likened to a rising dawn. As Yeshua's Bride, I am like a rising dawn that is growing in ever increasing brightness of faith and love. Keeping me eyes on Him makes me radiant!

Lord, teach me today to take my focus off negative things and put my gaze fully on You who gives me counsel and is able to do above and beyond what I could ask or think.

DAY 93

I AM A RELATIONSHIP BUILDER

Love each other with genuine affection, and take delight
in honoring each other. (Rom. 12:10 NLT)

I was created for relationship with God *and* others. Jesus is not a loner, so I am not a loner. But for any relationship to flourish there must be authentic love and honor. The Heavenly Father deems it very important how I treat my family, friends, and other relationships. I am to treat people with respect and genuine love. However they treat me, I am still to act in love and honor that builds, rather than carnality that tears down.

Satan works intentionally and craftily to separate family, friends, and a sense of safe community. He works through dishonor, impatience, rudeness, offenses, unforgiveness, control, gossip, betrayal, and abuse...to name a few. In God's love and presence, there is healing for the wounds I experience in hurtful relationships, as well as His wisdom, counsel, and fresh love for me in doing my part in building healthy relationships.

To love is to respect another despite differences. It is to celebrate their gifts and positions without jealousy. It is to show up in those relationships as someone who seeks to build another up and not tear them down, not ignore them, or dishonor them in any way, or use them to forward my own honor.

Jesus, You are a builder of relationship! Where do I need to build better relationships in my life with authentic love and honor?

DAY 94

I AM A RESTORER OF LIFE

Heal the sick, raise the dead, cure those with leprosy, and cast out demons. Give as freely as you have received! (Matt. 10:8 NLT)

I am given the charge from Christ to walk this Earth as He did and do the works He did of healing the sick, raising the dead, curing the leper, and casting out demons. Some today believe that what Jesus and the apostles did in supernatural healing and miracles is a thing of the past. They believe that God does not heal today. But that is not true; Jesus and Holy Spirit still heal! And want to!

Satan works to keep believer's powerless in their calling to be restorers of life. One tool he uses is false ideologies. The Apostle Paul called them deceitful spirits and doctrines of demons. If Satan can make me think I am powerless to do what I am called to do through Christ, then he gets a "go past go" card to continue his devilish work in the hearts, minds, and bodies of mankind. But I have received power and a commandment from the Lord to heal the sick and cast out devils, to restore life and remove death.

I must never look at sickness and say, "Oh well, that's it." I am to speak the Lord's dominion into the situation. God is able to do above and beyond what I can ask or think. And He desires to do it.

Father, what life around me needs Your supernatural restoration today in spirit, soul, or body?

DAY 95

I AM IN RIGHT STANDING WITH GOD

And having chosen them, He called them to come to Him. And having called them, He gave them right standing with Himself. And having given them right standing, He gave them His glory. (Rom. 8:30 NLT)

When Hashem chose me and called me to Himself in Yeshua, He did it with the purpose of giving me a right standing with Himself. With this upright position comes knowing His glory. It also comes with an incredible responsibility of position as His son or daughter. I am not standing in a corner like a shamed child or standing at a distance. I am not ignored, nor do I stand as a wall flower or one who is mute or deaf. I am standing right with God, and I have a voice and position for an effective work with a Holy Dad.

Abba, thank You for all You have given me in Christ to be an honored son or daughter in right standing with You. As I stand You put a royal robe around me, a ring of authority on my hand, and gospel shoes on my feet for walking in a heavenly calling on Earth.

DAY 96

I AM REDEEMED FROM THE CURSE

But Christ has rescued us from the curse pronounced by the law. When He was hung on the cross, He took upon Himself the curse for our wrongdoing. For it is written in the Scriptures, "Cursed is everyone who is hung on a tree." (Gal. 3:13 NLT)

I have been rescued by the hand of Love from a life that was condemned and under a curse. A curse is a decree sent with power to produce unfruitfulness, withering, striving, and lack in a person's life. Curses are real and operate where they have a legal right to do so. Sin gave the curse a legal right in my life. The cross and Jesus' blood satisfied the legal requirement needed to stop the curse, remove it, and restore blessing. I am not cursed; I am blessed and in Christ I have the authority to break every curse spoken against me…this is my heritage in Him!

As I take hold of the blessings in Christ, I command every curse from sin and generational bloodlines to be bound and depart from me. As I walk in the Spirit, I learn to not give any curse a right to come back through disobedience or ignorance. I don't give it any legal ground.

Yeshua, thank You for removing every legal ground for a curse to operate in my life. Thank You for the gift of repentance and restoration to break every stronghold and place where the enemy encamps to keep me unfruitful, striving, and in lack. Show me any place where I may still be giving demonic forces legal grounds of operation in me. Show me where I need to take authority over any curse. You want me to walk in full life and blessing!

DAY 97

I AM A SAINT

All Your works shall praise You, O Lord, and Your saints

shall bless You. (Ps. 145:10 NKJV)

In some religious circles sainthood is reserved for a special few. A board of men gather information and decide if the person (who is usually dead by this time) is worthy of this honorable title based on his or her good works. Had they faithfully lived a life that reflected being "set apart for the Lord"?

God, however, bestows this title on all who are in Christ. Those born of His Spirit are called saints, holy children set apart for Him. He calls out our identity as holy ones from the get go. The term saint means "holy one, sanctified, set apart." It is to be uncommon and have special or distinctive quality as opposed to what is common and without special value. The Apostle Paul admonished the Christians in Corinth for living "common" (worldly) as "mere men."

In other words, they were living like those who had no special value as lives set apart for God. They were still thinking of themselves in common ways and it reflected in a fleshly lifestyle. It was hindering them from living fully as a people who walked with a divine presence, and a Kingdom purpose. They didn't know who they were as a "Christ in me" people.

As a saint, I am set apart with special value. My life is uncommon and no longer my own to be lived as I want for myself and in worldly ways. I am consecrated to God; I am reserved for Him and His purposes, because the Spirit of His Son lives in me. Being a saint means I allow God to purify me from fleshly junk. This includes my thoughts, motives, and choices so I am free from anything defiling me as one who is reserved for a holy use. Trials, responsibilities, and chastening are all purposeful in shaping my life as one who is valuable and useful for Kingdom enterprises.

Father, what a great value You place on me in calling me a saint! Show me, today, any place where I am living commonly, and where You desire greater consecration.

DAY 98
I AM A SEEKER OF GOD'S KINGDOM

> But seek first the kingdom of God and His righteousness, and
> all these things shall be added to you. (Matt. 6:33 NKJV)

To seek first God's Kingdom is to put a priority on seeing the Kingdom of God manifest in my life and in every situation I encounter. It is to actively look for the supernatural wisdom, power, and intervention of God to be released into places where demonic oppression and sickness operate. This is how Jesus lived.

To seek first His righteousness is to put a priority on seeing God's justice at work against the unrighteous works of darkness. It is to seek true godliness in Christ rather than religious performance that stands in its own pride, self-will, and goodness.

Holy Spirit, teach me to prioritize my thoughts and desires regarding Father's Kingdom. Teach me to seek Heaven's presence and righteous justice, to see lives and cultures transformed by Your Kingdom. Let everything else be secondary to my life pursuits. Lord, where does Your Kingdom of light, life and healing want to manifest today?

DAY 99

I AM A SON OF GOD

For all who are led by the Spirit of God are sons of God.
(Romans 8:14 ESV)

In God, being a "son" is not about physical gender, but about having the life of the Son continually maturing me as Hashem's child. It means that I am learning to follow the leading of the Holy Spirit in my life, rather than following my own way of thinking. It is about a daily engagement with Father for taking an active role in the matters of His Kingdom. As I listen to Abba and follow His guidance, I make His desires my priority. I learn to put away childish things, grow in the knowledge of Him, and to conduct my life as a Spirit-led son or daughter who is here for a purpose.

Father, thank You for making me a son, not a slave, and for Your Holy Spirit who teaches me to walk it out in this life. Is there any place in my life where I am not listening to You or following Your leading, Holy Spirit?

DAY 100

I AM SEATED IN HEAVENLY PLACES

For He raised us from the dead along with Christ and seated us with Him in heavenly realms because we are united with Christ Jesus.
(Eph. 2:6 NLT)

As a believer I am seated with Yeshua who is sitting on the throne. What an incredible thought! To be seated with Him is a position of both rest and authority. In Christ, rest is not inactivity or sleep but refers to a position secured by Yeshua's blood that is free of death, bondage, chaos, and striving. My soul is at rest and I'm given a royal seat. The nails of the cross secured for me both rest and authority for the position I carry as Hashem's child and the Royal One's Bride.

I cannot fulfill divine purpose and govern Earth unless I am first royally seated with Christ in the courts of Heaven. Spiritual authority springs from above and rules the Earth, not vice versa. I can do a lot of good on Earth in practical ways, but until I am first seated in the throne room with Christ, I will not carry heavenly authority with His perspectives and counsel, as well as the royal decrees needed for overturning works of darkness.

Thanks be to God that this place is mine in Christ as a spiritual reality to be engaged with humility and boldness.

Yeshua, thank You for rescuing me from all places of unrest in my spirit and soul, and then seating me at Your side! Teach me the reality today of sitting with You to govern Earth.

DAY 101
I AM SENT INTO THE WORLD

As You sent Me into the world, I also have sent them into
the world. (John 17:18 NASB)

The word sent is "apostello," meaning apostle or sent one. I may, or may not, carry the mantle of an apostle, but as the body of Yeshua, the Apostle of my faith, I am apostolic in nature, and my gifts are given in link with an apostolic mission.

I am sent into the world to carry His presence and advance His Kingdom culture. And so He connects me with those who do carry an apostolic mantle since He has ordained apostles and prophets as the foundation for equipping His Body in apostolic Kingdom operations.

In Jesus' day, the term apostle was a Greek term referring to a Roman general who was appointed to go into a conquered region and establish the culture of the new ruling government. As a believer, I am sent to establish the culture of God's Kingdom in the Earth. His Kingdom presence manifests through divine miracles, counsel, peace, salvation and deliverance. It is a Father-centered Kingdom government. This is the mission I am sent with to minister to the world around me.

Abba, I will go where You want me to go, do what You want me to do. Your people will be my people. Your Kingdom come, Your will be done on earth as it is in heaven.

DAY 102

I AM SENT TO COMFORT THOSE WHO MOURN

He has sent me to…comfort all who mourn (Isa. 61:1-3 HCSB)

To comfort those who mourn is to ease the discomfort of one who is grieving. Grieving is a painful emotion we experience due to loss — loss of a loved one, finances, a home, position, or even the loss of a dream. There are many things we grieve over throughout life, but how we process grief is what makes a difference of it being a place we pass through or where we get stuck. All grief has stages that include denial, anger, sadness, letting go, and finding a new life after loss. Grief also has degrees of intensity depending on the type of loss and what it meant to us.

When a person gets stuck in the grief process they may stay in depression, anger, isolation, or be unable to let go, and thus they find difficulty moving forward. God wants to help those who are grieving to walk through their pain, to help them find the internal answers they need, and come out the other side into the light of hope.

People in grief often just need someone to listen to them as they process the pain or to help in practical ways until they get back on their feet again. When we are too weak to walk, we need someone to help us. God loves people and wants to help them. He wants to use me to help them and be His ministering presence to them.

Lord, who do You want me to walk beside today who needs strength and encouragement in walking through a season of grief?

DAY 103

I AM SENT TO HEAL THE BROKENHEARTED

He has sent me to bind up the brokenhearted…
(Isa. 61:1 HCSB)

To be brokenhearted is to feel like your heart has been crushed, rent apart, or shattered. Your heart is the center of your emotions, thoughts, passions, and understanding, and when these are crushed you feel powerless, even unable to move. You experience such a deep pain that you wonder how you will ever feel the same.

To bind up means to wrap firmly, to bandage tightly for healing. A person with a broken heart needs just that — someone to help hold their heart together until it mends. A person with a broken heart may tend to feel alone, as if no one can truly understand their pain or even care. But God cares. He sends me to wrap their heart with His love and presence, to be there for them while He picks up the pieces and puts them back together…just like how He sent others to help wrap mine with healing.

Lord, whose heart needs wrapping with Your love, today?

DAY 104

I AM SENT TO IMPART JOY

He has sent me to… to give them a garland instead of ashes and the oil
of gladness instead of mourning giving them a mantle of praise
instead of a spirit of fainting. (Isa. 61:1, 3 HCSB)

Another part of apostolic mission is to minister joy. The Apostle Paul said that while we weep with those who weep, we are also ministers of joy. After a night of mourning comes the light of morning. It is a new day, a day to be glad — the darkness is over and He has helped me. It is time to take off the robe of heaviness and put on praise. Praise energizes my emotions and revitalizes my thoughts with fresh strength and vision.

Sometimes it is hard to let go of sorrow if I have walked in it deeply and for a long time — it can become a "norm." But God does not want sorrow to be my norm. I may pass through the valley of the shadow of death but it is not my dwelling place. God well understands sorrow and His heart is moved by mine; He also affirms that in His presence is fullness of joy and that His presence is to be my dwelling place. He wants me to rise with joy that strengthens me for my journey as He works to remove the weight of sorrow. As I walk upright in joyful strength I am to minister His joy to others.

Father, thank You for joy! Help me to walk in joy and minister Your joy today. Your Joy makes my heart glad and my face to shine with a radiance that lights the world.

DAY 105

I AM SENT TO PROCLAIM FREEDOM

He has sent me to proclaim liberty to captives and freedom to prisoners.
(Isa. 61:1 HCSB)

A captive is one who is being held against their will, as one taken in warfare. There are different kinds of captivity — captivity in the mind and emotions (strongholds), intellect (philosophies), or even captivity of one's body (sickness or slavery). A prisoner is one who has been bound and imprisoned for a number of reasons or differing circumstances. No matter what kind of captivity I may find myself in, when any part of me is in captivity then so is the full range of my gifts, abilities, and God-given purpose.

God wants people free. He wants their destiny and calling freed from restraints, limitations and bondage. His Kingdom has come and He says that where He is there is liberty. Therefore, He sends me with His Word, presence, and power to proclaim freedom to those who are being held and restrained in darkness and injustice.

Lord, show me where and to whom You want me to go today and minister Your freedom.

DAY 106

I AM SHIELDED WITH FAVOR

For it is You who blesses the righteous man, O LORD,
You surround him with favor as with a shield. (Ps. 5:12 NASB)

A shield is a body protection during battle. We live in a world at war, a war between the kingdom of darkness and the Kingdom of Light. We need protection! We get assailed daily with dark thoughts, arrows to the heart, emotional assaults, and painful circumstances. We get assaulted in our finances, health, and relationships. Hashem says that part of His blessing on my life is that He surrounds me with His presence to protect my heart and life from the enemy's onslaught. I belong to Hashem; the enemy is not free to do whatever he wants.

Hashem's favor and acceptance shield's my mind from succumbing to those dark thoughts of fear and hopelessness that bombard me like darts to the heart. He sets His favor around me to protect my soul from sinking in despair in the midst of troubles and the challenges of life. Hashem is with me and will help me because He delights in me.

Abba, thank You for Your promise to help me, strengthen me, and support me in life. You do not leave me unprotected from the enemy, but You help me succeed in the life You have called me to.

DAY 107

I AM STRONG IN THE LORD

Finally, my brethren, be strong in the Lord, and in the power
of His might. (Eph. 6:10 KJV)

I am commanded to be strong in the Lord in the midst of life's battles, to lean on His everlasting power at work in me. I am not to be weak — weak-minded, given to doubts, having limited perspectives, or being weak-willed. I am not to give up or drop out. I am not to give in to doubt and unbelief when my faith is tested. I am to refuse the weariness that would overwhelm me, and to stand firm in His might. And sometimes that just isn't easy!

But God has strength to give me as I feed my thoughts on His words of truth, rehearse His words, and gird my emotions with praise. When God sent Joshua to lead His people into possessing their promises and inheritance from God, He instructed Joshua to be strong in faith. The way to be strong was to keep God's words in his mouth and mind, day and night, and be obedient to them. Only then would Joshua find success in his life and for his divine assignment — an assignment that impacted a nation's future (Josh. 1:7-9).

As I strongly hold to God's Word in my life, His Word strongly holds me. It empowers me for the battles I face and gives me strength for success. His presence indwells His words. Life is a battle, but in Christ I am made strong for living and for accomplishing the purpose for which God has put me here on this Earth. There is strength in His Word for my purpose.

Father, help me to be a lover of Your Word and to let its power be the source of my thoughts and words today. May I say what You say and not what another or my weaknesses tell me.

DAY 108

I AM THE SALT OF THE EARTH

You are the salt of the earth. (Matt. 5:13a NLT)

In the ancient world the value of salt was highly regarded because of its many valuable qualities. Salt was (and still is) useful in preserving food from corruption, for purification, and even for healing. In Jesus' day, it was acclaimed to be an important element for improving the quality of life in a society.

Jesus calls me to be salt in my society and culture. As an active believer, I improve the quality of life in my community and nation by my involvement and presence that carries Kingdom light and power. My active presence in community is important for preserving righteous values, healthy communication, and for keeping governing structures from becoming corrupt and defiled.

Without the presence of spiritual salt, nations quickly decay. Entities of governments, education and media fall into utter corruption, and thus comes the ruin of a society. This is what happens when salt has lost its flavor and becomes useless. I am not to be a useless Christian.

The spirit of the world wants to shut my mouth about Jesus, compromise my values, and be tolerant of evil. The god of this world wants me to deny my very conscience of right and wrong. That is because he, Satan, wants to destroy this world. But I am here as salt to enrich it, not destroy it. When I withhold my active engagement to preserve society, truth falls in the streets and lies are enthroned and the people fall into bondage under corrupt systems.

Abba, thank You for making me salt that enriches the lives of others and society — both spiritually and naturally — by being the presence of hope, love and truth. These enhance life and freedom in the way You intend. Where do You want me to enrich, enhance, heal, and preserve my community or nation today for the rich destiny they carry from You?

DAY 109

I AM A TEACHER OF NATIONS

Therefore, go and make disciples of all the nations, baptizing them in
the name of the Father and the Son and the Holy Spirit.
(Matt. 28:19 NLT)

To disciple means to teach and instruct. To go means to move, as opposed to not moving due to passivity, bondage, or death. As a believer, Yeshua charges me to move from where I am and teach cultures about Him and His words of life. I teach with words, in prayers, and by influence and involvement in community. I teach by the way I live.

Discipling nations involves Kingdom ministry to individuals, as well as to governing systems that impact or rule a society, whether a business system, family system, or civil system. To baptize is to immerse a person or people group into Jesus' death and resurrection. It is to facilitate the death of old corrupt systems and their governing structures, along with a resurrection of new life in covenant with God and His governing presence. It is to immerse these systems into the Father's nature, the Son's nature, and the Spirit's nature…for Their nature is in Their name.

Hashem wants the nations of Earth to be nations of life and light and not of darkness. He wants every tribe and tongue to know Him and to walk in their God-designed destiny.

Abba, I am an important part of Your nation-discipling plan. Show me how You want to use me in teaching and discipling my community, nation, or even another people group. Show me how to immerse them in the nature of the Father, Son, and Holy Spirit.

DAY 110
I AM TAUGHT BY GOD

I will instruct you and teach you in the way you should go;
I will guide you with My eye. (Ps. 32:8 NKJV)

There is a way that my life ought to go. There is a path upon which I am called to journey in intimacy with God. Jesus came so that I might be taught of the Holy Spirit how to walk that path. I am not forced to walk it, and it is why He calls it a path on which I am to be guided by His eye. It is a path walked in a face-to-face encounter with God, an eye-to-eye gazing. This can only be done through a life committed to walking in His presence and not at a distance. He doesn't want to have to jerk on my reigns as a rider on a stubborn mule. He wants me beside Him and my heart to move easily with His gaze.

The old nature of sin is like a mule that wants to do its own thing, but Father calls me to engage the new nature of humility that seeks His face continually. He desires a face-to-face engagement lifestyle with me. This is His method of teaching me as His child. In seeing His eyes I am able to capture His movement, as well as His heart-intentions and vision that are expressed through His eyes. God has a specific way for me to go, one that may not be what I naturally think or how He leads another.

Jesus told Peter to follow Him. Peter's response was to look at another and say, "What about him? What will he do?" Jesus told Peter that it was none of his business what the other would do. Peter was simply to follow the path that the Lord had for him.

Father, teach me to look at Your face and to follow the movement of Your gaze. Where are You looking today?

DAY 111

I AM THANKFUL

Enter into His gates with thanksgiving, and into His courts with praise;
be thankful unto Him and bless His name. (Ps. 100:4 KJV)

Being thankful is key to a life that thrives. It is a significant key to a lifestyle of the presence of God. Complaining, negativity, and ingratitude are the open door to sadness and for living a life scripted in hell. They are hell's worship hymnal.

Thankfulness encourages the heart, energizes the emotions, and lifts the eyes to see God, hope, and an expectation of good from Him. It places a focus on what I *do* have and what is good, rather than what is lacking or what is not good. It does not ignore what changes need to occur, but it does gratefully see the good that is present in life and that God will supply everything I need (Phil. 4:19).

Father, today I am thankful for Your love. I am also thankful for my family, relationships, work, abilities, and even the sunshine and the beautiful Earth You made. I am thankful for food and clothes, for water and finances. I am thankful for health and a sound mind. I am thankful for new insights and personal growth. I am thankful for the answers You bring me to problems and challenges. You are so good to me. Teach me to take all this goodness from You and help someone in need today.

DAY 112

I AM THIRSTY FOR GOD

As the deer pants for the water brooks, so pants my soul
for you, O God. (Ps. 42:1 NKJV)

King David said there was only one thing in life he cared about, and that was the presence of God. To thirst for God is to live in a reality of desire in which the heart can only be satisfied by God Himself, above everything else in this life…because He IS life.

God created us with a deep spiritual capacity of desire that seeks a certain satisfaction, one that can only be satisfied in intimate communion with Himself. The question is: where will my heart go to satisfy this deep longing within me? To God or to the spirit of the world?

Peter told Jesus, "Where else could we go? You alone have the words of life." Peter died for his willingness to follow Christ and his heart's desire for God. Paul, too, said, "For me to live is Christ, to die is gain." These men found that there is no other place in this world to satisfy the deepest desires of the human heart and soul but in the presence of God. And that satisfaction of communion with God is worth everything. "Let all who thirst come to the waters of life."

Father, let my one thing in life be to know You, to walk with You all the days of my life, and be satisfied in Your presence. Show me today where my soul is seeking to satisfy itself in waterless places apart from You. You alone are the fountain of life.

DAY 113

I AM A VISIONARY

Write the vision and make it plain on tablets, that he may
run who reads it. (Hab. 2:2 NKJV)

Being a visionary means to see an idea, concept, revelation, or insight. It is to see beyond what is naturally in front of me or to see something that has not yet been seen on Earth. Vision energizes me to pursue what I see, whether it involves something specifically for me, or for my family, community or nation. It might be a business idea or ministry calling. It is to see with the spirit and understand with the spiritual mind for active engagement in what God has given me to see.

Hashem told the prophet Habakkuk that a vision from Him, should be written down and not forgotten, even though it might take time to be fulfilled. Vision may come as a direct word from God, or as an "Aha!" moment, a dream, or a special insight. My engagement with God in prayer and life-choices regarding what I see in my spirit is critical for stepping fully into my calling and destiny in Him.

In Christ, I am given vision for establishing my path and setting me on a particular course. Scripture says that David served the purpose of God in his generation, that John completed his course, and that Paul had a race to run. These were men with vision of the heavenly task they were to engage in their years on Earth. Heavenly vision turns my eyes from the distractions of this world to focus on God and run with Him.

Scripture says that without vision we perish — we run around doing whatever instead of running with divine purpose for our life and generation. Whatever word, dream, or heavenly insight God has given me, I must pursue with faith, prayer, preparation and action, and allow it to shape me for my life and labor with Christ.

Lord, what is the heavenly revelation that You've given me that I am to run with You in life and glorify You?

DAY 114

I AM VICTORIOUS

But in all these things we overwhelmingly conquer through
Him who loved us. (Rom. 8:37 NASB)

I am an overcomer, a victorious one, a conqueror. I am not a victim, no matter what comes against me in life. I may be persecuted, accused, or even have been abused, but I am not destroyed. I may be pressed, but I'm not crushed to death. I may be perplexed but I am not driven to despair. Adonai is with me and I overcome through Him who loves me. I stand loved, cherished, and victorious in His might.

The battles in life I face are many, yet it is my mind and heart that become the battlefield upon which the war rages. What will I believe? Who will I believe? Will I believe that God will help me? That He is for me? That He loves me? That He has not forgotten me? That He is able to keep me and all that I have committed to Him?

In Christ, I am promised victory. I am not promised a bed a roses. Being victorious means I must take every thought captive and bring it to obey the Light of Christ's truth, love and power. There is victory to be experienced, no matter how things appear now.

Father, thank You for Your love that always teaches me to triumph. Where do You want me to triumph today?

DAY 115

I AM A WATCHMAN OF TERRITORY

Then the Lord God took the man and put him into the garden of
Eden to cultivate it and keep it. (Gen. 2:15 NASB)

To watch means to keep something safe by guarding it with the intention of protecting it and prospering it. A watchman is someone appointed to be attentive to what is happening in an area, seeing who is coming in or going out and what business they have there. When there is trouble approaching, a watchman calls out and warns the people to prepare and be armed.

A watchman of God sees and discerns the spiritual realm and the natural realm and what is going on in both. What is Earth doing? And more importantly, what is Heaven doing?

God created me to be His watchmen of the Earth; a calling that comes alive in Christ. Father puts me in a specific place with a charge to guard against enemy invasion (spiritual and natural) as well as to prosper it with His care (spiritually and naturally). I am not inattentive as I watch my home, community and region to know what is going on spiritually and naturally, who is coming in and going out, what kind of activities are going on, etc.

As I watch through prayer, God will speak to me about things, even hidden things. If an enemy is operating, I call an alert and bring in necessary others (God, people, angels) to overturn Satan's plan. Destruction comes when the watchmen are not watching.

Father, teach me to be a faithful watchman in my home and nation. Expose hidden things; show me where and how to take action.

DAY 116
I AM A WITNESS OF GOD

"You are My witnesses," declares the Lord, "And My servant
whom I have chosen so that you may know and believe Me and
understand that I Am He. Before Me there was no God formed,
and there will be none after Me." (Isa. 43:10 NASB)

A witness is one who testifies about an event. It is someone who has seen with the eye and heard with the ear firsthand what has happened. A witness is someone who was there and can testify to the truth of the matter.

I am a witness of God's love and power in my life. I have experienced firsthand His healing and delivering power. When I retell what God has done for me, I tell it as a first-hand eye-witness of what has occurred. I have seen Him work miracles in me and for me and those around me. I have seen it and known it to be real, not just a doctrine or an idea about God. There is power in my testimony because it is valid and not simply hearsay.

When I rehearse the power of God to another, there is power in my testimony that releases God's presence to effect the same miracle to happen again in the lives of those to whom I am speaking. A Hebrew word for "testimony" not only speaks of a re-telling, but means: do again!

Lord, show me who needs to hear today what I have witnessed You do, that they may receive a miracle, healing, or deliverance by re-telling of Your power to do it again!

DAY 117

I AM A WORSHIPER OF GOD

Come, let us worship and bow down. Let us kneel before the
Lord our Maker. (Ps. 95:6 NLT)

To worship is to humble myself before one I revere as a superior. It is to acknowledge with adoration the intrinsic worth of another greater than myself. It is to pay respect with honor through listening and obedience. It is to set my affections on the honored one as my priority in life. As a believer, I worship God alone. He is the Honored One. He is my Superior and my priority.

Worship is more than music; it is a lifestyle that involves the adoration of God in every area, activity, and expression of my life, and life's pursuits. I was created to worship God. I am a being of worship, and my worship makes place for the presence of who I honor. And so I am commanded to worship God alone.

Freewill, however, opens the door for me to either worship God or another entity. But in so doing, I must remember that who or what I worship will bring a presence into my life, whether of life or of death. I must choose wisely what door I open through worship. Hashem's presence alone brings life.

In the Garden, man chose to obey Satan and that worship brought death. Ever since, people have been worshiping false gods, gods of gold, gods of self, demon gods, and making a god of another person. And so death and brokenness covers the Earth. God wants His glory to cover the Earth, and it happens through worshipping Him!

The object of my worship is a choice about to whom I give my heart's affections, thoughts, and obedience. As my Creator, God is worthy of my affections. I express my worship of Him in everything I do by including Him in everything — in my music, business, arts, relationships, and activities that honor and glorify Him. The Father seeks those who will worship Him in spirit and truth.

Father, show me today any area where I may be worshiping another. Teach me to worship You alone for You alone are worthy of all worship.

DAY 118

I AM WASHED

And such were some of you. But you were washed, but you were sanctified, but you were justified in the name of the Lord Jesus and by the Spirit of our God. (I Cor. 6:11 NKJV)

Being clean is a beautiful thing! To be washed means that all the sin, failures, and junk of yesterday has been washed away by the soul cleansing blood of the Lamb of God. I feel light and free, nothing hanging on me. There is no reproach, lingering shame, or remaining agreement with evil. Jesus' blood has made me clean, wiped the slate, given me a fresh start with fresh clothes. The work of the cross and resurrection has given me a new beginning.

People might try to hold me in the frame of yesterday's dirt and failures, but God doesn't. He sees me as perfect in His perfect Son! I can stand confident in who I am in Christ as a clean one; the experience of His cleansing power can never be taken away. In Christ I have a new identity as being new, clean and whole. As a believer, I choose to see myself as He sees me, and live joyfully in His truth. I will not let the past hold me in an unclean place. I am washed.

Jesus, thank You for cleansing me! And that cleansing has released the blessing of God over my life!

DAY 119

I AM WONDERFULLY MADE

I will praise You because I have been remarkably and wonderfully made. Your works are wonderful and I know this very well. My bones were not hidden from You when I was made in secret, when I was formed in the depths of the earth. Your eyes saw me when I was formless; all my days were written in Your book and planned before a single one of them began. (Ps. 139:14-16 HCSB)

When Hashem put me together in my mother's womb, He fashioned me with intention. He picked out my nationality, my gender, my physical details as well as my personality and abilities. He gave me these for the work He has for me do in the place where He wants me on Earth. He even wrote a book about my life and all the wonderful things I would do and experience in relationship with Himself, His Son, and His Spirit.

God called me from eternity and wrote down my days before I was even born. He designed me purposefully in love. I am wonderfully fashioned for a radiant life in Him. I am not a heap of random parts without a reason or destiny. I am brilliantly made.

Abba, may I live out my days according to Your beautiful plan written for me. You have equipped me well for that plan with all You have put in me. May I develop fully for the days of destiny written in Your book. May the imprint of identity upon my very spirit, soul, and body come fully alive to glorify You. Use my gifts and all that You have given me as the story of Your life in me to be read by all.

DAY 120

I AM ZEALOUS

Even so you, since you are zealous for spiritual gifts, let it be
for the edification of the church that you seek to excel.
(1 Cor. 14:12 NKJV)

To be zealous means to be one who is eager, one whose heart and passion burn for something. As a believer, my heart burns for Christ. It burns to bring glory to my Father. It burns to be in intimate fellowship with Holy Spirit and to excel in every way for edifying the Church. I burn for reaching those in darkness with light, and to see Israel know Yeshua.

Yeshua Himself is zealous; He is zealous for Jerusalem; Yahweh is zealous for the fulfillment of His promise to His people. He is zealous against her enemies for they are His enemies. It is said that He puts on zeal as a cloak and that His zeal will establish justice in the Earth. Psalm 69:9 prophetically speaks of Yeshua's zeal for the house of God that burned in Him as an unstoppable passion; God's house is the place of His glory, where Heaven meets with Earth to reconcile Earth back to Himself.

If God is zealous, then I must be zealous with His passions. I must be zealous and not passive in my walk with Him…zealous to grow in gifts that edify others. Zealous to reach souls for Christ. Zealous to restore my nation to God. Zealous to see Israel see their Messiah and return to Hashem.

God's Word instructs me to "Never be lacking in zeal, but keep your spiritual fervor, serving the Lord. Be joyful in hope, patient in affliction, faithful in prayer. Share with the Lord's people who are in need. Practice hospitality" (Rom. 12:11-13 NIV). To "keep" my spiritual fervor means to guard it from waning, for there are many things in life that work to distract it, dilute it, and steal its holy fire. I am to guard my heart's passion in following close to Christ for the life I am intended to live in serving Father, His Kingdom, and the world in which I live.

Holy Father, set me on fire with holy passion! Let me run my race on Earth with passion and not passivity, with divine counsel and not worldly compromise, with wisdom and not whining. May I live my life with purpose and not purposelessness. So be it.

WRITING YOUR OWN DECLARATION

As you have read through these "I am" statements, I pray they have quickened your understanding in new ways regarding who you are in Christ. Abba Father wants you to walk in the fullness of your Kingdom identity.

I encourage you to take a walk through the Word of God and write down any other "I am" statements as the Holy Spirit shows you. Or, it might be something different that doesn't begin with "I am…" such as, "I can do all things in Christ who strengthens me," or "I will bless the Lord all my days."

Write what Holy Spirit shows you and declare it! Let the power of divine declaration break any stronghold of false identity you may have carried. Let the declaration of His truth about you strengthen you and ground you in the likeness of Him who has loved you and called you for such a time as this.

I am…I can…I will…

_____

_____

_____

_____

_____

_____

_____

_____

_____

_____

.

www.ingramcontent.com/pod-product-compliance
Lightning Source LLC
Chambersburg PA
CBHW070817050426
42452CB00011B/2082